Praise for *Live You*

Just the title alone speaks volumes. When one considers the challenges, obstacles, pressures, and demands that accompany so many children as they walk through the entrances of their schools every day, it becomes obvious that on the other side of those doors MUST be educators who strive to live their excellence while they simultaneously bring their best selves to school every day. In this follow-up to his phenomenal book *Culturize*, Jimmy Casas digs even deeper, with a particular focus on the individual teacher. He offers invaluable advice and strategies on how to consistently bring the best "you" while always maintaining a focus on your "why."

—**Baruti Kafele**, retired principal, education consultant, author

Shifting from a culture of compliance to one that puts human understanding and grace at its center is a challenge to the centuries-long top-down hierarchical structures that have shut out the voices that can make our educational systems the best they can be. In *Live Your Excellence*, Jimmy Casas puts humanness at the center. His highly relatable stories resonate and show how we can grow from frustration to understanding and embrace opportunites that help empower the voices that create a positive culture.

—**Pam Gildersleeve-Hernandez**, executive director, CUE

In *Live Your Excellence*, Jimmy Casas does it again. He writes as only one who has lived and breathed the work of a true educator can. He cuts through the noise—the endless initiatives and failed "fixes" for education—and perfectly captures the heart of what truly moves our schools forward: our relationships with each other.

—**Amy Fast, EdD**, high school principal, author, and education commentator

Live Your Excellence is a beautiful testimony to the power of investing in others and going beyond compliance in the interactions that we have each and every day with both our colleagues and students. If you want to reflect on your work both personally and professionally so that you can grow not only yourself but your school, read this book. Jimmy nails it with *Live Your Excellence*.

—**Hamish Brewer**, award-winning principal and author

The gold of *Live Your Excellence* isn't in what's new, it's in what's *nuanced*. That's no insult; for educators, this book is a blessing. I was ready to order it when I read Jimmy Casas's advice to a principal about long-standing sore points in his school such as bus duty, recess duty, lunch duty, and morning duty: instead of treating these merely as duties, Casas suggests, regard them as opportunities to build relationships. It's one of the best suggestions I've heard for shifting thinking around tasks that have too often been considered burdens. Casas has an eye for providing new lenses for the work educators are already doing. His insights facilitate practical applications, positive outcomes, and, most importantly, paradigm shifts in thinking.

—**Ken Williams**, author, speaker, coach, status-quo disruptor, Unfold The Soul, Inc.

You will find yourself reading this book again and again. Jimmy Casas reminds us all why we choose to dedicate so much of ourselves to making a difference in education. The prompts that conclude each chapter are guideposts in the journey of bringing our best selves to the forefront of our work and lives. A truly great book that deserves space on your bookshelf and in your heart.

—**Denise Murai**, school parent and community liaison, HundrED ambassador, HundrED.org

In *Live Your Excellence*, Jimmy Casas continues to focus on the most critical aspect of education: school culture. Blending practical expertise and tips that challenge your thinking as a teacher or principal with heartfelt stories that will leave you yearning for more, *Live Your Excellence* compellingly addresses both the art and the science of education. Jimmy fearlessly tackles the issues in schools no one wants to think or talk about, the dangerous undercurrents that form when we're afraid to have the hard conversations. A conventional response to these dangerous undercurrents would be to make people *comply* with "the rules." This book will lead you down another road, one that takes you to a vibrant, thriving school culture where students and staff *invest* in each other because of an intense commitment to relationships. A must-read for all educators who desire to have a greater impact on their students!

—**Jay Scott**, secondary school redesign specialist, Kansas State Department of Education

Jimmy Casas reminds us that we have not set out on this journey to be average. The personal stories in this book will prompt you to pause and reflect upon your own practices. You will be challenged to shift your mindset when responding to difficult situations. Most importantly, you will discover that it's the relationships that we build every day with our students, colleagues, administrators, and families that matter most! *Live Your Excellence* provides the foundation to building a positive school culture where everyone helps, encourages, and guides each other toward their personal excellence.

—**Sharyn Kish**, 2020 Ohio Teacher of the Year, District 5

Live Your Excellence will have an immediate impact on your school culture. This inspiring read reinforces Jimmy's impact as a thought leader, influencer, and model for our work to transform lives through the art of education. *Live Your Excellence* is a must for those interested in leading from the heart.

—**Aaron L. Polansky**, superintendent, speaker, and author

Live Your Excellence is one of Jimmy Casas's best works! He offers the reader powerful examples of lessons learned from his lengthy career in public education and provides solutions to navigate the challenges of school leadership. Jimmy's humble and vulnerable approach embraces the value of building and cultivating relationships at all levels.

—**Jerry Almendarez**, superintendent, Santa Ana Unified School District, California

In *Live Your Excellence*, Jimmy Casas takes the ideas of Culturize deeper to help educators move from a culture of compliance to an investment-based culture. Casas shares how important it is to invest in what is best for students and for you—even if it means being vulnerable and sharing mistakes. This book encourages you to consider that learning is more than academics, relationships are not something you can outsource, and challenging ourselves to do what we ask students to do can motivate us to change. Through personal stories that will touch your heart, reflective questions, and insightful strategies, Casas demonstrates how to discover your WHY so you can strive to thrive and *live your excellence*.

—**Barbara Bray**, speaker, podcast host,
and author of *Define Your WHY*

Educators want solid, workable solutions to the challenges they face in leading a new generation of students, and *Live Your Excellence* by Jimmy Casas truly delivers. With laughter and relatable stories, Jimmy reminds us of the need for personal accountability by admonishing us to bring our best selves to school every day. While that might seem simple, educators—particularly "seasoned" ones—can easily become complacent if they are not careful. *Live Your Excellence* is full of encouragement and provides a necessary "reboot" for every level of school leadership.

—**Kevin D. Newman, EdD**, superintendent,
Manassas City Public Schools

Good education books offer both pragmatic strategies for implementation and compelling stories for inspiration. Jimmy Casas delivers both in *Live Your Excellence*. This book is a clear roadmap for investing in children, peers, and ourselves so that a culture of excellence, positivity, and success can take hold. Jimmy's love for students and educators is undeniable. Do yourself and your community a favor by taking the time to read this book. We will all be better for it.

—**Weston Kieschnick**, author, speaker, and senior fellow, ICLE

From the first compelling anecdote to the last memorable lesson, Jimmy Casas takes us on an authentic journey in his latest book. *Live Your Excellence* is an intensely honest look into investing in, influencing, and improving a school community in order to inspire others to bring and give their best. Deeply personal and universally relatable, *Live Your Excellence* makes you want to stand up, stand proud, and risk taking the next step in your own personal journey of fulfillment.

—**Jennifer Bloom**, principal, Lower Elementary School,
New Hope-Solebury School District

LIVE YOUR EXCELLENCE

LIVE *Your* EXCELLENCE

Bring Your Best Self to School Every Day

Jimmy Casas

This book is available at special discounts when purchased in quantity for educational purposes or as premiums, promotions, or fundraisers. For inquiries and details, contact the publisher at books@daveburgessconsulting.com.

Published by Dave Burgess Consulting, Inc.
San Diego, CA
DaveBurgessConsulting.com

Cover design by Chad Beckerman
Interior design by Liz Schreiter

Library of Congress Control Number: 2020932543
Paperback ISBN: 978-1-951600-08-2
Ebook ISBN: 978-1-951600-09-9

Dedication

To my three children, Aj, Miraya, and Marisa. You continue to be my inspiration for doing my best to live my excellence every day. Your mom and I are so proud of the three of you and hope in some small way that we played a part in shaping you into the kind, caring, generous, and beautiful young adults that you are today. Love you with all of my heart.

The greatest glory
in living lies not
in never failing
but in rising every
time we fall.

–NELSON MANDELA

CONTENTS

LIVE YOUR EXCELLENCE

INTRODUCTION

WHEN YOU KNOW YOUR WHY YOUR WHAT HAS MORE IMPACT BECAUSE YOU ARE WALKING IN OR TOWARD YOUR PURPOSE.

—MICHAEL JR.

As soon as I saw Antwan's face, I knew he was upset. Antwan had been a frequent flyer—a regular visitor to my office over the course of the school year. But this time he seemed more agitated, more animated in his breathing, and his body trembled as he stood in the doorway.

"Talk to me, Antwan. What happened?" I asked. Antwan mumbled underneath his breath over and over, "She's fake. She's fake. Ugh. I can't stand Ms. Silver!"

"It's OK, Antwan. It's OK," I repeated over and over.

"No, it's not OK," Antwan shouted as he fell to the hardwood floor in my office and began to sob. "Ms. Silver lied! I hate you all! You lie! You tell us that you care, but you don't. You are all fake!"

More than twenty-five years have passed, and yet I can still remember the anger in Antwan's face, see his tears flowing, and hear his voice trembling as he struggled to catch his breath. For years, I couldn't let go of his words. I didn't want to. To this day, those four simple words—you are all fake!—serve as a reminder to me of how some students can view the adults in their lives.

It's true that Antwan was frustrated, hurt, and struggling to articulate his feelings in a way that would have helped him in this situation with Ms. Silver. But the truth is that for some of our students our actions *are* fake. As educators we must never forget that—it's what happens when we ignore the impact our words and behaviors can have on our students.

Ms. Silver had been frustrated with Antwan for quite some time. He was wasting class time, disrupting class, and not completing his homework. Worst of all, he was keeping others from being able to do their work and preventing her from teaching the other students.

In an effort to turn things around and win Antwan over, Ms. Silver cut a deal with him. If he behaved in class and turned in his assignments for the week, she would reward him with tickets to a Milwaukee Bucks basketball game that Saturday. And it wasn't just any game. It was against the Orlando Magic, who, at the time, featured Antwan's favorite player—Shaquille O'Neal.

In Ms. Silver's mind this was just the right carrot to get Antwan to do his work. And it did seem to work. Antwan buckled down and did his work, and with each passing day of the week Ms. Silver praised Antwan and his efforts to the rest of the students. On Thursday, she contacted Antwan's mother and grandmother to update them and make the necessary arrangements to take him to the game. On Saturday they saw Shaquille O'Neal and the Magic play against the Bucks. By all accounts, it was a wonderful night.

So why was Antwan in my office on Monday? As he described it to me, Ms. Silver became frustrated when he arrived in class without his homework completed. She wasn't as nice as she had been on Saturday when she stopped by to pick him up, and according to him, she quickly got angry and told him that she was disappointed in him.

Antwan's description of Ms. Silver wasn't off base. As Ms. Silver related to me later, she *was* frustrated by his behavior after the previous week's success—especially because she felt she had made a connection with him at the game over the weekend. Ms. Silver confirmed to me that she'd lost it when he arrived without having completed a single problem on his assignment. But it was what she said next that sent Antwan over the edge:

> After everything I did for you Antwan, this is how you thank me? I took you to dinner and a basketball game and paid for everything out of my own pocket, and you disrespect me by not doing your work? You used me to get what you wanted, and now you've gone right back to the way you were. Well, don't ask me for anymore help or for anything else. *If you want to fail, then go ahead and fail. I don't care.*

And just like that, the damage had been done. Ms. Silver was fake. I was fake. We were all *fake.*

As I sat with Ms. Silver after school that day discussing what had transpired with Antwan, I could see the despair and guilt on her face. She felt like she had failed Antwan. She was disappointed in herself. And worst of all, she really did see herself as a fake.

But she wasn't the only one that felt like a fake. I wasn't just being called on to rebuild a tattered relationship between a teacher and a student but repair the psyches of both as well. I was in my first year as a principal, and seeing her completely torn apart, I realized that nothing in my educational background had remotely prepared me for this situation.

. . . .

Years later, I was faced with one of the most challenging and heart-wrenching incidents of my career: the death of one of my students days away from graduation. As teachers and school leaders—as people—at times of tragedy, we can become consumed by pain and feelings of guilt. We begin to question what, if anything, we could have said or done differently to prevent such a terrible loss from occurring.

Even later, I remember a moment I had with a teacher in Lake Tahoe, Nevada. I had just given a presentation, and after I spoke, a teacher approached. She shared with me how she was struggling with the loss of one of her students. Her eyes teared up as she described the emptiness and the guilt that she felt inside. She wanted to know what she could do to get past the sorrow of having lost someone to suicide.

How can any of us ever be prepared to handle such a loss? Truthfully, I don't think we ever can.

When tragic events occur in our school communities, all of us—school leaders, counselors, teachers, and support staff alike—are quickly thrust into difficult situations. We're forced to navigate a very delicate and emotional time for not only the family who is suffering from the loss of a child or loved one but also for various members of the school community who are experiencing their own grief. Teachers and administrators must not only be prepared to give an immediate response but one that's caring, compassionate, and respectful. At the same time, they must address the emotional needs of a student body and colleagues who are all affected in different ways. It's a challenging position for any leader or staff member to have to step into.

The work of an educator comes with a plethora of challenges. And while resolving Ms. Silver's well-meaning mishandling of a student interaction is miles away from responding to the tragic loss of a student's life, both situations remind me that most of what we deal with cannot be taught. No amount of schooling or advanced degrees can ever prepare you to deal with a colleague weeping in your office at the thought of having failed a student—and certainly not the sight of an empty chair in your classroom.

But after all of these experiences, I was determined to not feel so helpless moving forward.

• • • •

If you are still reading this, maybe—just maybe—it's because you get it. You know this struggle all too well. You've been there. You've experienced these same feelings, or you've sat with a colleague and heard similar feelings expressed. And maybe you yourself have felt at a loss about how to respond.

I honestly believe Ms. Silver's intentions were sincere. But still, both she and Antwan were left frustrated, hurt, and struggling to communicate in an effective way in order to help themselves in this particular situation.

Sometimes we expect all students to have the necessary skills to be able to communicate their feelings in a respectful way, but in reality they may not yet have developed the level of maturity needed to work through their struggles on their own. When we hold them to a standard they can't reach, we are setting *ourselves* up for failure and frustration.

That's because when we fail to make the impact with students that we so desperately hope to, we are at our most vulnerable and most at risk of losing our focus. And the same is true for school leaders who want to help their staff in such moments—it's easy to lose perspective and criticize the actions of a teacher instead of focusing on the rebuilding that needs to happen.

Ms. Silver didn't want to fail, but yet there she sat lamenting how she had managed her relationship with Antwan. Truth be told, she had done the best she knew how—just like many of us do when we walk into school each day. I certainly tried my best that day as I offered her advice for how to move forward. And yet we both left feeling like we were fakes, with Antwan none the better off.

. . . .

Throughout my career I've replayed that incident many times, rolling it over in my mind's eye to see it from all angles. But the question I've not been able to answer is this one: Why is it that we are so hard on ourselves? What leads us to question our ability to inspire our kids the way we had hoped when we first started teaching?

Could it be that Mrs. Silver needed to let go of what happened and give herself a bit of a pass? Should I give myself a pass for not knowing how to help her? Don't we all deserve a pass every now and then? It's not like we walked in one day and said, "You know, I think I want to mess up as a teacher." Were any us really prepared for what lay ahead of us when we walked into our own classroom for the very first time?

It's not only teachers who face what seem to be overwhelming challenges on some days. Administrators often find themselves in a similar position. Were they really prepared for the complexities of what principals are often expected to navigate?

And why stop there? What about bus drivers, secretaries, paraprofessional educators, custodians, and other staff members who are all doing the best they can with what they know? None of them want to settle for failure. And yet, all of us end up too often feeling underequipped to succeed.

It's a question I keep coming back to: How did we all wind up feeling so *lost*?

In the twenty-five years since Antwan broke down in my office, I've come to appreciate an all-important truth: when we lose our *why*, we lose our *way*.

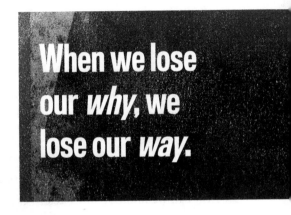

When we lose our *why*, we lose our *way.*

No one goes into this profession to be average. We just slowly gravitate there over time. We are all susceptible to it. We're unprepared for the complexity of what we face, and we just get lost. And when we're lost, average tends to rear its ugly head. It happens in those moments when we are tired or frustrated. It happens when we begin to think we can no longer make a difference.

Do you remember when you sat down to be interviewed for your job? Do you remember what you said? Did you say, like many educators do, that you wanted to be a champion for all kids?

What happened to that teacher who couldn't wait to go out and make a difference in the lives of our precious children? What happened to the teacher who walked into school each day believing they could inspire others? What happened to make them feel like a failure? And worst of all, to feel like a fake?

Have you reached a point where you are praying for a snow day just so you can catch your breath and get a little reprieve from the daily grind? Or worse yet, have you reached the point where you are beginning to resent kids rather than cherish them?

You are not alone in having these emotions. Ironically, many of our kids have the same feelings every day in the schools they attend—feelings of isolation, loneliness, and a complete disconnect from their peers and the adults.

I am not judging you. I get it. I really do. One day you just wake up and realize you're there. And it's a shitty feeling.

So where do you go from here?

. . . .

This book attempts to help you as an educator find a way to rediscover yourself in order to bring your best self to school every day. Too often teachers and administrators—like Ms. Silver and myself in the incident with Antwan—feel like we are faking it or like we're just getting by. How do we find a way forward and reconnect with the core values that once made our work so much more than average? How can we find our way back to excellence?

The answer is that our school cultures need to change. We need to move from a culture of *compliance* to a culture of *investment*.

It is my belief that most of the issues we are facing today in schools are the result of the adults acting and responding in ways that too narrowly focus on compliance. Working in education is hard, and even the most committed educator, over time, can be brought to the point where they're just doing what they need to get by. That becomes to be what their administrators ask of them, and it ends up being all they ask of their students: Leave your baggage at the door. Do what you have to. Comply. This leads to average—at best.

But in order for education to succeed, to be more than average, educators must move past doing just enough and remain committed to improving—themselves, each other, and their students. What does investment mean for educators? It's honestly engaging with your own strengths and shortcomings, committing to improvement, and putting yourself on the line. A whole school of educators with the charge to understand, appreciate, and embrace our own deficiencies rather than to deflect or defend our responses and behaviors so that we move beyond our shortcomings with humility is a school with a culture of investment.

Only by embracing our challenges will we create investment-focused school cultures that reflect our most cherished values. A change in culture can provide what we need to make a difference at every level in a school:

- Staff members can develop skills to create an investment outlook in our students—so no student ever has to experience the feelings that Antwan had in my office.
- School leadership can support staff in adopting a perspective of investment—so no one ever feels the way Ms. Silver felt in my office.
- Educators can rekindle the sense of purpose we once had and get back to making a difference by embracing an investment mindset in our schools—so we can all find our way back to excellence.

In the pages that follow, I will share insights and experiences that I believe are vital in helping us on our journey to not just *talk* about excellence but to *live* our excellence. Behind these insights is a belief that that the culture of schools needs to change in order for the individuals within them to stop feeling "fake" and authentically flourish.

I start by sketching out a philosophy for excellent schools—one that embraces investment over compliance—and spells out how such a philosophy takes hold in a school. In it, I illustrate the kind of decision-making process that educators who embrace such a philosophy use to arrive at answers that create a collaborative culture of investment in schools.

In the next section I turn to look at how excellent leaders approach students. From dealing with tardiness to classroom instruction, I look at how to change and manage our interactions with students to avoid negative undercurrents and create a school culture of investment.

The third section of the book examines interactions with colleagues. It discusses the need for avoiding divisive interactions and valuing the contributions of everyone. I look at ways we can better navigate hard conversations through an investment mindset that reflects our passion for excellence.

The final section of the book turns inward and investigates the kind of changes individuals need to make in themselves to rediscover their excellence. From recalibrating our approach to difficult conversations with staff members to examining our capacity for leadership, this section calls on educators of all stripes to invest in themselves by caring for themselves as the foundation for a healthy school culture.

At the end of each section I include reflective questions designed to assist you in taking an inventory of your current culture and challenge you to take the next steps towards excellence.

The purpose of this book is to inspire all educators—teachers, administration, and support staff—to re-examine their thinking in order to bring the best of themselves to school each day and what in their school cultures might be preventing that. I hope to illustrate not just how our own shortcomings unintentionally impact school culture but to inspire real and honest conversations that dive deep below the surface and provoke a community of educators to embrace steps toward becoming more invested in our schools.

Will it be worth it? Yes! Our children and your colleagues need you—at your most healthy and vibrant—to do this critical work. I am sincerely grateful that we have passionate people like you who are committed to living your excellence every day!

Reflecting on Excellence

- Ms. Silver's focus was on getting Antwan to comply. How would you have worked with him differently? How does that reflect your excellence?

- Describe a time in your life when you lost your way. What did you do in order to find your way back? Are there any parts of your personal or professional life where you are starting to feel like you are getting lost? What is one thing you can do today to begin to find your way back?

- What is holding you back from living your excellence? From being the best teacher or principal? What's keeping your school from becoming excellent?

PART ONE

A CULTURE OF

Investment

YESTERDAY I WAS CLEVER,
SO I WANTED TO CHANGE THE WORLD.

TODAY I AM WISE, SO I AM CHANGING MYSELF.

–RUMI

Chapter One

THE COMPLIANCE TRAP

I still recall the day I jumped up on a cafeteria table out of frustration.

I had already caught myself using a harsh tone with students who walked away without cleaning up after themselves. I had grown tired and frustrated with students in the cafeteria during lunch. I am not exactly sure why, but on that day it became personal.

What exactly bothered me so much? Was it that I thought our students were being disrespectful to our custodians and kitchen staff or that they seemed so entitled that they thought it was somebody else's job to clean up after them? Admittedly, I have always had a soft spot in my heart for the custodial staff who work in our schools, especially those who take a tremendous amount of pride in keeping our classrooms, hallways, bathrooms, and other areas clean. Maybe it's because my father served as a school custodian, and so did I too. All I knew at that moment in the cafeteria was that what I was seeing had to stop.

Along with the assistant principals and cafeteria supervisors, I was set on getting these students to comply. We used the PA system to announce to students that they needed to clean up after themselves.

We walked from table to table telling them to dispose of their trash. We kept an eye on students who we suspected were leaving trash on the tables. Nothing seemed to work.

Our conversations became harsh. My comments about our students also started to influence my colleagues in a negative way. I directed our school resource officer to monitor the cameras so we could identify the culprits and then gather them up and bring them back to the cafeteria where we assigned them clean-up duty as a consequence for not cleaning up after themselves. Desperate to try something different, we offered to let the students leave the cafeteria early—something they often requested—but only if they had cleaned up after themselves.

Looking back, I realize I had fallen into the compliance trap: my approach was not genuine. It was conditional. Everything I did was only to get the students to comply. I didn't involve the students. I didn't sit with them or ask questions to better understand their perspective or have meaningful conversations. I didn't take the time to get to know them as kids—as the good kids they were. Instead, I barked orders, assigned seats, and took away privileges.

I wasn't investing in the students. Rather than take the time to partner with them or give them a voice in resolving this concern, I found myself jumping up on a cafeteria table. Not only did I yell at hundreds of students for not cleaning up after themselves, but I grabbed a trash can and tossed garbage all over the cafeteria floor to prove my point: this is how they were treating our kitchen and custodial staff each time they expected them to clean up after them—like trash.

As I reflect back on that day, I am able to see where it all began to go wrong. I just missed it in the moment. I had approached this dilemma the only way I knew how at the time: by punishing those who weren't following the rules.

I was reminded of this experience about a year ago when I came across this reflection by Tom Herner,

If a student doesn't know how to read … we teach.

If a student doesn't know how to swim … we teach.

If a student doesn't know how to multiply … we teach.

If a student doesn't know how to behave … we punish?

This is exactly what I had done. I punished the students for their behavior. Making the kids spend a week cleaning up after everyone else did not teach them a lesson. Yelling at them didn't help. It made them resent me, resent their teachers, resent adults and authority figures.

In the years since, I've seen and heard things like this over and over again in my travels around the country. Educators are doing the best they can with what they're taught to believe is true: that punishing kids when they don't follow the rules is what we are *supposed* to do. We often fall victim to believing that kids need to "understand that there are consequences for their behavior" because this is the way the "real world" works. When you don't follow the rules you will be punished, and eventually you will learn not to make the same mistake again.

This mentality hurts not only our kids but also the educators who work in schools. We end up creating a gotcha culture rather than an I've-got-you culture. A culture of *compliance*.

But there's a better way.

What we should be trying to do instead is to create cultures of investment where both the students and the staff are doing the right thing because in their hearts they believe it is the right thing to do—not because someone else insists they have to. We can begin to cultivate a healthier environment, where everyone in the organization carries themselves with a sense of pride and a commitment to being the best version of themselves.

How Cultures of Compliance Get Started

A school principal recently confided in me about his struggles to get his staff to comply to certain things he expected them to do. When I asked him to share an example of his experiences, he told me a story of how he was frustrated with his staff for failing to stand outside their classrooms and supervise the hallways during passing time on a daily basis. He had been clear and even asked nicely. Initially his staff complied, but over the span of a few weeks, he noticed less and less of them outside their classroom doors until eventually there was hardly anyone to be seen.

Frustrated, he sent out an email to the staff reminding everyone of his expectations and letting them know he would be monitoring them. The next day staff could be seen standing outside their doorways again. Unsurprisingly, he told me the impact of his intervention was temporary. His frustration grew more intense, and within a couple of weeks, he finally reached a breaking point when an altercation between two students took place in a busy hallway near several classrooms. Fortunately, no one was hurt, but the principal had had enough.

The next day at a faculty meeting he voiced his displeasure with his staff and told them that moving forward he would be monitoring the hallways even more closely. Any staff member who was not out supervising between classes would receive at minimum a written warning followed by a letter of reprimand for repeat violators.

Principals getting frustrated with staff. Teachers and bus drivers losing their cool with students. Over the course of my career I've learned that there are ways to minimize these encounters so that they don't get out of control.

Authoritarian cultures are rooted in compliance. You see this in workplaces where a staff has learned to do what the boss tells them to do—or else! These same roots begin to dig their way into classrooms and wrap themselves around teachers who then begin to behave in a similar fashion, commanding kids about what to do and ready to offer up a detention or a written office referral for those who don't comply.

Why Mindsets Matter

The first school I ever worked in was a magnet school for the arts for students in grades six through eight. It was located in downtown Milwaukee. It was still under construction the first day I walked in to work and came complete with an asphalt parking lot that also served as a makeshift playground. It didn't take long for me to notice the bars over the exterior windows and the metal detectors when I entered the building.

I was given a tour of the building's five levels: a basement and four floors. My classroom was located on the fourth floor, but I learned that it would not be ready for the start of school so my room was relocated down the hallway in a small auditorium. Rows of desks had been situated on the stage, and a temporary black-board on wheels had been provided. To say I was disappointed was an understatement.

Further impacting my mood and attitude was the nonclassroom duty that had been assigned to me—cafeteria hallway supervision. Besides my under-construction classroom and the auditorium, the fourth floor also housed the cafeteria. That meant that every student in the building headed up there for lunch. For sixty minutes every day, I was responsible for supervising the hallways and helping keep order for 650 middle schoolers, most of whom I did not know and, truthfully, did not want to know.

I can tell you I did not embrace my new role in a positive way. In my mind, it was enough for me to be responsible for my own students, and I didn't understand why I was forced to "babysit" kids who regularly snuck out of lunch and roamed the hallways, causing issues and disrupting classes. I saw it as an extra responsibility and—quite frankly—a burden. Rather than embrace my role and try to interact with students, I glared at kids who stepped outside the rules. I barked orders, yelled, wrote referrals, and, on a few occasions, even chased a few students who were trying to escape down the stairs. To say I was miserable is putting it mildly.

At the time I thought I was doing what I had been asked to do: keep order in the halls. I was focused on what many of my college instructors had told me during my coursework and what the teachers had shared with me during my student teaching. I was supposed to maintain order, be firm but fair, and demand respect from the students or they would walk all over me.

Flash forward four years later, and you might wonder what happened to this negative young teacher. I was fortunate to be influenced by some exceptional teachers and mentored by some passionate leaders who eventually helped shape my thinking and perspective in a positive way. Over the next twenty plus years, my perspective would continue to be shaped with each experience, through observations, discussions with students, encounters with staff, and personal interactions.

One thing that I've learned is what I was given on the fourth floor of that building in Milwaukee wasn't a burden—it was an opportunity. Research tells us that the foundation of healthy and positive cultures is the way we interact with others through relationships that are fostered on trust. Positive interactions—a friendly smile, a warm hello, a pat on the back, a simple conversation—can have effects that multiply throughout the educational experiences of every student and teacher.

Had I shifted my thinking back on the fourth floor in Milwaukee, could I have done my part to support my colleagues and administration in positively impacting our school climate and culture? Would I, as a teacher, have benefitted? Would the students I was entrusted to watch over have been better off? Today, I believe the answer to those questions to be yes, without any shred of doubt, but I didn't back then. I just didn't know any better.

Now I know that the culture of compliance that I contributed to—and was affected by—came at the cost of hurting the overall climate and culture of the school.

Positive interactions among students and staff happen in many schools today, but unfortunately, rarely at the level they should. Too often, we fail to follow through consistently on a daily basis.

We must continue to challenge thinking and influence behavior that we know causes us to fall short of making a positive impact on all kids. On the days when you are supervising students, try to avoid defining it as hallway duty or lunchroom duty, playground duty, or bus duty. Instead, begin to see all of these as relationship opportunities. Shift from seeing your responsibilities as burdens, and open yourself to opportunities.

The Compliance Trap

Sometimes when we discipline students we react in a negative way when we don't get the change in behavior we want, and that can trap us. Not all students react the same way to consequences. Quite frankly, neither do adults. See if you can relate to this scenario.

I recall a student, Ian, who had been giving me a difficult time in class. I tried several different interventions and eventually decided it was time to contact his parent. I and his parent agreed that Ian

> On the days when you are supervising students, try to avoid defining it as hallway duty or lunchroom duty, playground duty, or bus duty. Instead, begin to see all of these as relationship opportunities.

should stay after school as a consequence of his recent behavior, but more importantly, so I could get to know him a little better and help him get caught up on his work. The result was everything I hoped for. Ian was back on task, he seemed more focused, and he was getting his work done. He felt good about his effort, the parent felt good about his work, and I felt great about his progress.

A few weeks later another student, Devon, was demonstrating similar behaviors, so I decided to follow the same process as with Ian. Again, everyone was satisfied with the results. I began to think that I had figured out the formula for working with disruptive students in class.

And then along came Patrick. I followed the same process as before, feeling confident that I would turn Patrick's behavior around. But it didn't work. I started thinking, "What is going on with Patrick?" Sure that I had the right formula, I again repeated the same process and sets of interventions that worked with Ian and Devon, but my efforts seemed futile. Patrick wasn't responding. Slowly but surely I began to resent Patrick as my patience ran thin.

This was the moment of truth, and it's where I failed many times. I blamed Patrick. After all, my interventions had worked with Ian and Devon, so logically they should have worked with Patrick. But they didn't. So I convinced myself that the student was the problem—that I was right and he was wrong. (There were even times I would share with parents that it was evident that their child was the problem because the other students had responded appropriately.)

What I failed to recognize in that moment was that I was the problem. You see, I made an assumption about Patrick by believing that he should have responded the same way as Ian and Devon, rather than recognizing that Patrick was not Ian or Devon. Patrick was Patrick. He needed a different set of interventions, responses, and conversations.

I needed something different too. I needed a greater skill set, but I also needed a different mindset, one that allowed me to understand that not all students (or adults) are going to respond the same way to my interventions, supports, or expectations just because they worked for somebody else.

Too often, we believe we know what to do, and that if we do the right things and have good intentions, we will always get the same positive results from our efforts. It doesn't work that way. What does work is remembering that all students are unique, special, talented, and have gifts. It's our responsibility as a group of talented, caring, and educated adults to make the necessary changes in our thinking to adapt to the needs of each individual student and do everything possible to instill in them the belief that they can be successful. They'll only believe that if we believe it.

We differentiate for academics, but sometimes we don't consider differentiating for student discipline, even when we know not all students will respond in the same manner to the same interventions. An investment mindset that sees students as having assets that need to be tapped instead of limitations that have to be overcome means that we must be prepared to try a different approach for each individual.

Chapter Two

WHERE TO START WITH A CULTURE OF INVESTMENT

I encourage you to recalibrate your mind and begin to think in terms of investment, rather than compliance. What I've gleaned from my experience over many years as a teacher and building leader is that cultures of compliance are not sustainable or healthy for any organization. We want our culture to be vibrant, stimulating, and rooted in the idea that values come from a place deep down in people's cores, not from an external force or mandate.

People do best when they believe what they are doing is the right thing to do. That is the root motivation of excellence. They don't need someone to tell them to conduct themselves in a certain fashion. They have too much pride and care too much not to. It is who they are.

As I grew in my role as principal, I learned that in order for my staff to become invested in the very things I believed to be pillars of a strong culture, I had to be invested in them.

So, if I, along with the assistant principals that I was mentoring, was going to expect the staff to supervise the hallways to the high standards that I expected, two things needed to happen. First, I needed to define what I meant by supervising. Did I want the staff to have all eyes on students looking for any wrongdoing, or did I want them actively engaged and interacting with students in a genuine manner in order to foster positive relationships (with all students, not just "their" students)?

Second, I had to be prepared to invest in the staff the same way I expected our staff to be invested by standing and engaging them in the hallways or when they entered a faculty meeting. I had to be prepared to stand at the entrance of the school and every meeting and greet each teacher and staff member, engage them in conversation, share a friendly hello or handshake, offer a word of encouragement, and provide an empathetic ear—just as we expected them to do with students. After supporting each staff member in such a way, I would no longer have to tell staff what to do.

> **There's a better chance that our expectations will be met if we model the behaviors we hope to see.**

We ask, encourage, or even expect others to do things, but there's a better chance that our expectations will be met if we model the behaviors we hope to see. Won't our words be more impactful and resonate more deeply if they are supported by our actions?

Investing in others means taking genuine and active steps to build relationships using our own time and attention. By setting clear expectations and modeling them with sincerity, we show that they are generated from our core values, not arbitrary demands that others only comply with because it is what we tell them to do.

Just Hanging On

I once had a discussion with a teacher who was feeling frustrated with some members of his administration. "What is it specifically that is bothering you?" I asked.

"I feel like they've checked out. Like they are just hanging on for the next few weeks until the end of the school year. They keep saying 'We'll come back to that next year.' Next year? It's frustrating because we've made a lot of progress and there are still things we can do to keep moving in the right direction this year. I don't want to just hang on. I want to keep getting better. If we don't, then what is the point of coming to work? We wouldn't tolerate that from our students, but it's okay for us to shut down?"

It's not uncommon for me to hear similar comments from administrators when I've asked them how they are doing.

It's April. How do you think I am doing?

Just trying to make it through the next few weeks.

I'm tired. My teachers are tired. The kids are tired.

When I hear these responses, I can empathize. There were certainly times when I felt like I just needed to "hang on and get through it." I convinced myself that it had been a long year or I had worked hard and deserved a break or that whatever we needed to accomplish could wait until next year.

This mentality doesn't just crop up at the end of the year. The weeks leading up to Thanksgiving, December holidays, even spring break—as soon as school starts, we sometimes feel desperate to get to the next long weekend or extended break.

But listen to the comments of the teacher again.

I don't want to just hang on. I want to keep getting better. If we don't, then what is the point of coming to work? We wouldn't tolerate that from our students, but it's okay for us to shut down?

As I reflect back on his words, I know that teacher was right. We would never accept such an attitude from our students. Sometimes we can be overly critical of our kids, failing to recognize that we face the same issues they do.

Do you see the disconnect between the administration's response and that of the teacher? Not only are they not on the same page, I am not sure someone with a just-hanging-on attitude could even see what's causing the teacher's frustration. Yes, there are some teachers and administrators who feel at times like they are just hanging on, but there are also just as many educators out there who not only feel like they still have a lot to give but are *ready* to give it. A teacher who wants to improve is a golden opportunity for an administration hoping to build capacity. But when the administration turns down the opportunity to invest in him, he becomes frustrated and sees his administration as shutting down. Situations like these create an undercurrent of complacency that damages the school's culture. It becomes clear to both students and educators that a school like this is not a place for growth.

Rather than let them get swept away in those undercurrents, how can we recognize students and colleagues who are still pushing forward while changing the mindsets of those who are just hanging on?

Start by inviting your colleagues or students to be a part of the work you yourself are focusing on. A culture of investment is created when everyone knows that their contributions are valued. To that end, it's important to work side by side with others as partners to model the importance of planning, learning, and investing together. It's all about empowering others.

Then, you have to keep them involved. Communication is key: update anyone who will participate or will be affected by your work. Meet regularly, monitor progress, and ask for feedback. Ask questions and create opportunities for others to share their ideas. You shouldn't be afraid to ask for help, and when you do, be sure to show that you're willing to accept the input you've solicited. Including others' perspectives in your work encourages them to invest in solutions with you.

Of course, it's always important to manage time well. Begin by recognizing that regardless of how much time is left in a school year, we can decide to keep making progress. However, we must understand that folks have a reason to be tired at the end of any school year, so prioritize one specific area that together you can invest in.

Most of all, celebrate your successes together. Validate the work of those involved with a personal and sincere acknowledgement of their work.

It is easy to get stuck in a just-hanging-on mentality. I know this from personal experience. Yet as invested educators we must not adopt attitudes and behaviors that we would never accept from our students. Rather than just hanging on, what if we *let go* and began to think about our school culture differently? What if we realized that every moment contains the same promise that the beginning of a new year does?

The Cycle of an Educator's Year

Each August signifies a new beginning, a fresh start to the school year, and for some, maybe even a newfound hope to erase the memories of an exhausting and stressful end to the previous year. You bring a certain energy, a level of enthusiasm, a readiness to make an impact in the life of a child. I am guessing that some of you went out and purchased a new outfit for the first day of school, or maybe laid out your clothes the night before and then mumbled to yourself that you had nothing to wear—all because you wanted to bring your very best to the kids whose lives you aim to impact. However, any educator who has served in this profession for more than one year can tell you that there are ebbs and flows, a certain rhythm to the cycle of a school year that will take you on a journey of ups and downs from August until May (or June for some of our comrades). I've tried to illustrate what this cycle might feel like in the poem I have written below.

In August you walked into school every day energized because you couldn't wait to see the kids and give them a high five or a fist bump as they walked into your classroom.

In September you greeted your colleagues with a smile, and when they asked how you were doing, you told them you were great.

In October when they asked how you were, you hesitated and told them that you were fine and that you were doing okay.

In November your pace was considerably slower as you walked into school, your energy lacking a second gear.

In December your smile had been erased from your face, rarely greeting others as they walked by, your voice barely audible when you did.

In January you were begging for a snow day, already in need of time off even though you had just returned from an extended break.

In February your tone was harsh and your patience thin and you began to question your commitment to your students and colleagues, wondering if you could still make a difference.

In March you could see the rays of the sun peeping through your window, giving you a renewed sense of hope.

In April you were back to your old self, interacting with students and staff, telling them to have a wonderful day.

In May you were embracing your kids, telling them how much you were going to miss them and how you wished you could do it all again.

So I ask you, why can't every month look like August and May?

Adopting an Investment Outlook in Student Interactions

The shift in approach to a culture of investment also requires thinking differently about how we approach student interactions. Let's take a more methodical look at what that entails.

Instead of trying to change the behavior of others, what if we began to try to influence their thinking so they change their own behavior? Think of this as coaching, rather than "dealing with," others.

Imagine a scenario where an assistant principal leaves his office after having just met with an angry parent over their son's suspension for vaping in the boy's bathroom. As he walks out into the front office he is told that Cody, a student who has a reputation for getting in trouble, is waiting to see him. A teacher has reported that Cody was in possession of a small pocketknife in class. The assistant principal, still frustrated from his interaction with the parent, addresses Cody in a way that makes his short temper clear and directs the student into his office. When he asks Cody where he got the knife, Cody says that he found it. The assistant principal doesn't believe Cody. He tells Cody he doesn't have time for stories and that if he won't tell him where he got the knife, then he will be suspended from school and he can deal with the police. Cody then tells him his father gave the knife to him.

Students and staff can discern when our levels of frustration rise. Maybe we become short in our responses, our tone no longer carrying the same level of patience and kindness. Slowly, we begin to separate ourselves from them; this works against us long term. Over time, students will begin to resent adults who respond to them in this manner.

Now imagine the same scenario, but this time rather than direct Cody into his office, the assistant principal sits next to him and in a concerned voice asks how he is doing. After listening to Cody, he asks a couple of follow-up questions to gauge his mindset. He then invites Cody into his office and tells him how much he cares about him and that he is a little worried about him. When he asks Cody where got the knife, Cody responds that he found it. But rather than become impatient, the assistant principal maintains a positive approach. He asks Cody more follow-up questions because he is truly concerned for his well-being and his propensity for finding himself in bad situations. Eventually Cody says that he got the knife from his father, but then he adds one more piece to the puzzle. His father and mother don't get along. If his mom finds out his dad gave him the knife, Cody is afraid it will cause another argument and he won't be allowed to join his father the following weekend for a hunting trip.

It's true that in both scenarios, the assistant principal was able to get Cody to tell him where he got the knife. However, in one situation the student felt trapped, and in the other, he was supported. When we are confronted with a dilemma, the way we approach the situation can change more than the outcome. The way we manage ourselves and the level of sincere investment in our every interaction with each student will eventually determine how they view

Our every interaction with each student will eventually determine how they view the adults in their lives.

the adults in their lives. How we are defined is often based on how we respond in the moment.

Rather than react with resentment, invest more by seeing the good in students. Ask questions to better understand their perspective and gain more knowledge before responding or making a decision. By responding in a genuine, curious, and sincere way we make progress—even if it's slow progress. Patience will be required.

Chapter Three

WHAT AN INVESTMENT MENTALITY ENTAILS

Approaching Change with an Investment-Based Mindset

If you want to move your school to an investment-based culture, you need to start laying the groundwork for that change now. And one of your biggest decisions will be how you work with your colleagues to carry out that change.

Change can bring about an array of emotions, thoughts, and feelings. We've all been there. Perhaps our minds and bodies were filled with anxiety, nervousness, fear, or worry. Maybe we were left frozen, unable to act. Or maybe those emotions were embodied in excitement, energy, or a celebratory feeling of hope and newfound inspiration. In many cases, I've had a combination of these feelings.

It is not uncommon to hear people describe change as difficult. In fact, we often describe change as something that people hate, fear, or just don't like. We think about it. Other times we talk about it. And too often we just keep thinking about it or even talking about it, and we don't *do* it.

One night I was listening to a podcast on schools when I heard a guest share his views with the host on the topic of change. One particular comment caught my attention. He shared that if school leaders are to be successful, they must expect their teachers to work collaboratively in teams. He went on to say that schools where teachers operate independently of each other are more likely to fail than their counterparts.

His comments made me pause. His insistence that collaboration was a necessity was a clear example of a compliance mindset. I asked myself if it had to be an either-or proposition. Are there not times in our work as educators that situations cannot demand both collaboration and independence? What's more, a leader with an investment mindset would focus on helping to develop their colleagues' strengths—not forcing them to follow a particular model.

In the highly collaborative world we live in, it can feel as though we have stigmatized those who prefer to work alone to the point we now hesitate to work independently for fear of being viewed as not a team player. Think of the impact of this type of thinking on students in the classroom. Have we stigmatized some of our students for feeling this way?

Some in our profession are critical of those who want to work independently, as though these individuals are somehow isolating themselves from others. On the contrary, there is a difference between working independently and working in isolation. Those who learn independently, for example, are still influenced by outside sources that often lead them to a broader perspective and deeper understanding.

Given a task, timeline, and clear instructions, I believe professional educators can choose to work on their own or collaboratively with colleagues. Sometimes they may need to combine the best of both methods to meet their needs when the time calls for it. At times it will appear as though they have exhausted their moments of independence. They may revert to working collaboratively or vice versa, moving back and forth effortlessly, depending on what the situation calls for in that moment.

Sometimes they'll just need fresh experiences or surroundings. Depending on the situation and context, they might want to approach a task from the mindset of independent workers in collaboration or collaborating individual operators. It might be important to be independent in one moment yet collaborative in the next.

Whether they are working in content or grade-level teams, partnering with instructional coaches, taking part in exchanges with other school districts, or using digital tools to connect with others around the country, I would argue that in the end both students and educators need to make a place for both the way "I do it" and the way "we do it."

Investment-Based Decision-Making

Those in leadership roles usually have a pretty good grasp on their current situations. Either through their own experiences, observations, or conversations with others, they are able to ascertain the realities around them. They know where their strengths and challenges lie, and they do their best to address them. Most leaders have also figured out where the land mines are buried and do their best to avoid them for fear of creating a disruption that can be hard to recover from.

As a principal, I, too, was pretty good at getting the lay of the land at any given moment. However, I often found myself chasing my tail when it came to what I wanted the future to look like for my organization. This was because I had never been taught to think about processes, frameworks, and systems. I certainly had never been given the tools to lead in an investment-based manner.

Instead, twelve years into my career as a principal, my approach to leading was more like picking the flavor of the day. I gave my attention to whatever came across my desk or whatever idea a staff member shared with me at that very moment. The result was chaotic, inconsistent, and more often than not oriented to compliance-rather than investment-based solutions. It never crossed my mind that I should consider changing my process for making a decision. After all, I was the principal, and I thought I should just make the decision that I thought was "best" for all involved—without ever questioning what "best" looked like. At the time it seemed an effective way to manage the plethora of decisions that needed to be made. From a coaching perspective and in my work today taking inventory of school and district cultures, I am able to see things now that I was never able to see before when I was living it in the moment.

One day as I was coaching a principal named Tom and shadowing him on his rounds through his building. It was seven in the morning, and the building was quiet as we approached a side door where a teacher had just entered with two students.

"Good morning, Karen," Tom said.

"Good morning," Karen responded. "I know that we aren't supposed to let students in before seven thirty, but they were cold, and I just felt that I shouldn't leave them standing out there freezing. I get here every morning at seven, and there are always kids out here. I will be honest: I just let them in. Are you okay if I just keep doing that rather than let them freeze?"

Tom responded hesitantly, "I guess that would be okay. Some of the staff have complained about kids arriving too early and roaming the halls, but you are right, it's too cold to leave them out there. I will let security know to start unlocking the doors at seven."

And just like that, a new "policy" had been established.

I understood why Tom had made this decision. It was in the best interest of students. The weather really was too cold for students to be standing outside. He had solved the immediate problem, but he had failed to look at what was best for his school's future. His decision at that moment was made with good intentions, but it would eventually create issues for his staff and in turn for him. Simply put, he took the easy way out rather than follow an investment process for making his decision. Instead, he made it in the moment and in isolation. In doing so, he strengthened the currents of compliance swirling underneath the surface of his school's culture.

Can you see how? Karen shared the story and told some of her colleagues that Tom was now changing the time for student access to the building. When the kids were stopped in the hallway for being in the building before seven thirty they told a staff member they had been given special permission. Rather than rolling out a new policy in an orderly way, Tom had set up a train of gossip that quickly spread throughout his building—comments, questions, and complaints about Karen, Tom, the kids, the lack of communication, about how no one ever knows what is going on around here because the rules are always changing, blah, blah, blah! Ultimately staff morale took a hit. Tom had enforced his decision, further strengthening the school's culture of compliance.

What Tom needed was a process to support him in consulting with the other stakeholders so that decisions with the potential to affect the entire organization would not be made in isolation. Tom didn't see the need; in fact, he later blamed the staff for being negative. After all, he had made a decision that in his mind was in the best interest of the kids. He couldn't understand how the staff could be upset about a decision well within his prerogative. I don't think most were. What they were upset about was that he had changed the rules halfway through the game and not only hadn't included his leadership team (they had originally agreed to seven thirty after much deliberation) in his decision but also failed to communicate the change to anyone.

Imagine for a moment how the outcome could have been different if Tom had approached the situation from an investment-based perspective. Tom might have responded with something like this:

> Thank you Karen. I love the heart you're showing and thank you for looking out for our students.
>
> Students, I am going to go ahead and let you enter this morning because I can tell you are cold. However, I am going to ask that you come to the office with me. Right now doors open at seven thirty because we don't have any supervision until that time when staff arrives to work.
>
> Karen, I am going to share your idea with the building leadership team and discuss some ways in which we can allow for students to enter the building earlier during the cold months while also providing appropriate supervision. In the meantime, feel free to share your concerns with your colleagues so they can also see your perspective based on your experience this morning. I will follow up and get back to you. Thank you for always looking out for the well-being of our students.

Although I would consider this decision minor, it serves as a good reminder that, big or small, every decision we make or fail to make as leaders has the potential to impact both school culture and morale in positive or negative ways.

Many educators know what they need to do in the moment, but without an investment-based outlook, they may struggle to carry their vision beyond the current moment.

Every decision we make or fail to make as leaders has the potential to impact both school culture and morale in positive or negative ways.

Chapter Four

INVEST IN YOURSELF

I n my work today coaching teachers and principals in school districts across the United States, I encounter educators every day who aspire for greatness. Not just for themselves, but more importantly, to provide hope and inspiration for others so they too can experience being a part of something great. To never settle for good enough.

Like many educators who continue to do this noble work, I was naive enough to think that I could do it all by myself, first as a teacher then as a school leader. After all, I had the drive, the ambition, the passion, the energy, and certainly the work ethic to do it my way.

Early on I was committed to do whatever it took to find success in my work, but I paid a heavy price. How foolish I was to think I didn't need anyone's help. Both my health and my family suffered, and yet I ignored it, because after all, I was committed to the students and to my staff.

The truth? No one was taking care of me, including, well . . . me.

I haven't forgotten what it feels like to skip breakfast, skip lunch, consume a jar of bite-sized Snickers bars or M&M's, proceed to snack on a bag of popcorn and a Cherry Coke, and then inhale as much food as possible on arriving home after a twelve- or fourteen-hour workday. Not quite exactly a diet for a healthy heart, I know. But it happens to many of us. And sometimes we even fall into the trap of speaking of a mismanaged diet as a badge of honor.

There's got to be a better way, a more logical approach to each day than running around trying to accommodate every student, every request, complaint, and every need that comes along. For the first twelve years in my role as a principal I struggled in this area. I honestly thought it was what I was supposed to do: to take care of everyone else's needs, regardless of the toll it took on me. Isn't that why I became an educator? To help others, to serve them in a way that made them better?

This may sound good in theory, and perhaps it has even served you well up to this point, but if truth be told, I don't think you can sustain it for very long. And if you try, you are going to pay a dear price.

Dr. Jody Carrington, in her book *Kids These Days*, reminds us that we must first look after ourselves before we can be in the right frame of mind to take care of the needs of our students and staff. More often than not—to our credit—we are so laser focused on providing the necessary care to the children in our care that we neglect our own needs.

This isn't always because we have too much to do. Sometimes it's the result of a lack of preparation, organization, or prioritization on our part. We cover up our defaults by labeling them as a "sacrifice" for the kids, our boss, or the job. Too often we are willing to sacrifice our own personal needs for the needs of others to the detriment of our bodies, our minds, or our own emotional well-being. After a certain period of time, this self-neglect begins to affect not only our own well-being but that of our loved ones at home.

How often have you found yourself easily irritated by something at home only to realize you were able to manage a similar experience at school with patience and kindness? How is it we can be better with other people's kids than we are with our own? Or kinder and more forgiving with peers at work than with our own spouse? I know what it feels like to turn into someone who you not only don't recognize but don't even like. That behavior in turn begins to define your culture at home.

So invest in yourself. Don't neglect your health, your sleep, or your relationships. Begin to behave your way to a more joyful outlook. Here are a few things to try:

- Smile. Smile. Smile. Smile as often as you can.
- Be grateful and share your gratitude with others.
- Ask someone else, "How can I help?"
- Write a kind note.
- Go for a walk without technology.
- Visit a friend or family member.
- Make travel plans.
- Cook a meal.
- Listen to an audiobook or a podcast in your car.
- Exercise for fifteen minutes.

Only by investing in yourself will you have the energy and mindset to truly invest in others.

Reflecting on Excellence

- What are the practices or behaviors you expect from your students and staff? Are you modeling the same practices or behaviors?

- Where is your school on the compliance-investment continuum? Where would you place *yourself* on that continuum?

- What steps are you taking to ensure that you are intentionally investing in others?

- Can you think of a recent interaction that reflected a compliance outlook? Can you rescript from an investment perspective?

PART TWO

REACHING

Students

**DO THE BEST YOU CAN UNTIL YOU KNOW BETTER.
THEN WHEN YOU KNOW BETTER, DO BETTER.**
–MAYA ANGELOU

Chapter Five

SO GLAD YOU ARE HERE TODAY

E very day hundreds of opportunities pass us by. We just don't see them. One of my greatest regrets over the course of my career is thinking back on how many opportunities I left out there. How many times did I choose not to interact with a student? Countless.

One evening I received an email from a former student of mine. It literally brought tears to my eyes.

I had tried to engage her in conversation one October day several years ago and in doing so, something took me aback. The look she had given me seemed harsh, almost one of disgust. I didn't know why. I was perplexed. I did not recall having any prior interactions with her. I didn't recognize her, which bothered me even more, especially since I prided myself on being a champion for students.

I asked a counselor to find out who the student was because I couldn't shake the feeling that something was not right. After learning her name, we researched her permanent record and noticed she had been in our school only two weeks. We learned that she was seventeen years old, had transferred schools *nine times* during the course of her schooling, and had earned a total of five credits. In the notes there were comments indicating no parent contacts, even though several attempts had been made.

Over the next several months we took many steps to try and learn more about her. Some things were very clear to us. Her attendance was near perfect, but she was not completing work. She was guarded in her interactions and responses with others and rarely spoke, and not a single teacher, counselor, or adult was able to connect with her on a more than superficial level.

I struggled to figure out how to help her. We tried several interventions to try and learn more about her story. Counselors, social workers, nurses, administrators, therapists, and even the police tried to intervene, but to no avail. My attempts to interact with her left me feeling hopeless. The Department of Human Services refused to open a file on her because, in their opinion, there were no safety concerns for her well-being: she was coming to school regularly and there was no indication of physical abuse. On three occasions I attempted a home visit, but I was never able to get anyone to answer the door.

I found myself hesitating, not sure what to do. She wasn't unlike other students I encountered during my career who seemed to want adults to stay away from them. She certainly did not want to have anything to do with me. It felt as though she wanted me to give up on her. The situation brought back a ton of emotions from my own school experience. I too gave others the impression that I wanted them to leave me alone, while inside I wanted them to not give up on me.

I decided not to attempt to approach her and to keep my distance, but I did my best to let her know I wasn't going to quit on her. The only thing I did was greet her without looking at her every time I saw her in the hallway or cafeteria. In the morning I would only give a simple "good morning" or "so nice to see you." In the afternoon, I'd say, "So glad you are here today." At the end of the day, I'd say, "Hope you had a good day" or "Be careful going home tonight." I just didn't want her to think that we had given up on her. I wanted to her to believe that, regardless of whatever interactions she'd had with school figures in the past, we would always be there for her.

And then one day in late April, I learned that she had withdrawn from school. I was devastated. Disappointed that I'd known full well that something wasn't right but was never able to convince others that we needed to do more. Angry that I hadn't done more myself.

I would think of her often, wondering what came to be of her. Was she in school? Was she safe? Was she finally able to connect with someone? Over the course of the next year there were moments I would think of her. And then slowly, as time passed by, she became a distant memory. And then, five years later, one early evening I received an email that hit me in the gut. There I sat staring at my computer and immersed in her letter.

> Mr. Casas, I don't know if you remember me or not, but my name is Savannah. I am writing to you today because my college professor asked us to write a letter to someone who made a difference in our lives, and I thought of you.

I sat there trying to recall our interactions, but I couldn't point to a single one that I could say made a difference.

> I want to thank you for never giving up on me even though I gave you every reason to do so. I want you to know I heard your voice, and some days that was the best part of my day.

By now tears were flowing down my face.

> I am doing better. I have been in therapy for over two years. I am sorry I was so disrespectful back then, but I hope you can forgive me. My father was doing horrible things to me, and every time I saw you, all I could see was his face laying on top of me.

And just like that I lost it. I slumped back into my chair, sobbing uncontrollably.

I share this story to remind you that investing in our students matters. It matters more than we may ever know. Even the simplest of words can leave a lasting effect. But it's not just our words. When you are intentional in your interactions with others or give your time to listen to a student or colleague, you have the potential to leave a lasting impact that you may not even realize in the moment.

Relationships are not something you can outsource to someone else. Every day there is a young girl or young boy walking the halls feeling invisible. You have the opportunity to bring them into the light, and a responsibility to shift your mindset so that you begin to see those hallways as pathways for your excellence to shine through. By investing in relationships with students and colleagues in more meaningful ways, not only can you impact their lives but, in turn, they can change yours.

Relationships are not something you can outsource.

Chapter Six

REMEMBERING WHAT IT'S LIKE

There are days that I struggle with my self-confidence. Put me on a stage in front of hundreds of people, and I won't blink an eye. Introduce me to a sport or any activity that requires some form of athleticism, and my swagger comes out. Invite me to a podcast, and I can talk for hours. But ask me to take an exam of any kind, fill out a tax form, or write a paper for a graduate class, and I'll wilt and fall like a leaf dropping from a tree in late autumn.

What is it about writing that causes many of us to hesitate or lose our confidence? I've contemplated this a lot, and I am not sure that there is just one answer. I think it's personal to each individual. What holds you back? What is it that really holds me back? Sometimes I'm disappointed in myself. Other times, embarrassed or even angry. Maybe it's fear that holds me back. But fear of what?

Maybe it's a fear of stirring up old memories that I don't want to think about or, worse yet, relive. Why recall those elementary years when I struggled to read and write and was constantly being pulled out of class to work one on one with an aide.

Or junior high, when after three weeks of school I was removed from my language arts class for being a constant disruption and placed in the in-school suspension room for the rest of the school year. Yes, you heard me right. I only had three weeks of language arts in the seventh grade. I am not begrudging the teacher at all. She did the best she knew how with a kid who was often disrespectful and had a chip on his shoulder. I am not bitter with the vice principal, Mr. K, who told the teacher not to worry because she would no longer need to deal with me. He too did what he thought he needed to do at the time: support his teacher.

And don't even get me started on high school. After missing the entire year of language arts in the seventh grade, I never recovered. I felt like there were too many gaps to overcome and thought I didn't stand a chance.

So here is where I've landed. Sitting here trying to get the words out for this book. I've been here before. Self-doubt can leave me feeling unsettled, even paralyzed. I feel stuck. And it scares me. I hate this feeling. So why do I keep coming back?

Then it hits me. Isn't this the same feeling many of our students are experiencing in schools today? I am guessing you've seen it too: students doubting themselves, lacking confidence, scared, and paralyzed too. Like many of you, I've shared their struggles in these moments, and I'm pushed to reflect on them.

So, that's one thing many of us as educators have in common with many of our students. When it comes to writing, the struggle is real! So real that is causes many of us to shy away from it or avoid it all together. When was the last time you had to write a paper? Have you ever written a blog post? How about a book? If you are one of those who has worked hard at your writing or invested a lot of time in reading and writing, good for you. Perhaps think of another task that you had to do where you weren't quite as confident in your skill set and try to remember how it made you feel.

Take for example blogging. What percentage of teachers and principals currently have an active blog? A tiny fraction, I'd say. We can offer an abundance of reasons why more educators are not blogging. One that I hear often from educators is they don't think they have anything profound to share. Can you imagine? *Educators* don't have anything profound to share? Imagine saying to your students, "Class, I just need you to know that throughout this course I will not be sharing anything profound. Everything I share with you will be something you've heard before." Sounds crazy, huh?

Does it make us better at what we do when we can empathize with what our students are going through? I think so.

Think about this. Every day when students walk into school, at some point they are expected to write. At times we get frustrated with their efforts (or should I say lack of effort). Some students shine, and we highlight their efforts, and others just do the bare minimum. Who faces the biggest challenge? Those who truly lack confidence and cannot get themselves to write anything for fear of looking stupid.

We ask students every day to do something that many of us haven't had to do for quite some time. The truth is I worry that we have forgotten what it feels like to be a student and the anxieties that came along with it. I know Mr. K wanted to support his teacher. I just wonder how things would have been different for me

> **We ask students every day to do something that many of us haven't had to do for quite some time.**

45

if he would have remembered what it was like to be a student and supported me too.

Maybe that idea should motivate us going forward: by doing things we fear or struggle with, we can remind ourselves what it feels like to lack confidence. That can serve as a bridge to help our students experience the one thing so many of them need to believe in themselves—a sense of accomplishment.

Looking beyond Academics

As we look back and try to remember what it was like to be a student, let's not forget the obstacles beyond academic struggles that our students face. Many—maybe most in certain schools—face challenges that are much greater than just overcoming their fear of writing.

There is a luxury many of our children who grow up in privilege take for granted: that an adult will be there to get them up, lay their clothes out, prepare their breakfast, pack their lunch, and help them gather their things before driving them to school or getting them to their bus on time. These students can have their issues too, but I want to talk about the daily challenges many of our students without these supports face.

Often we are tempted to point the finger at students for failing to live up to our expectations. Take for instance the issue of tardiness. Every day in schools across our country, students arrive later than they are expected to class. We have labeled these infractions as tardies. As far back as I can recall, tardiness has been an ongoing issue in schools. In fact, I would argue that the biggest infractions regarding school discipline fall in the attendance and tardy arena. Tens of thousands of students fail to comply with their educators' expectations every day.

Have you ever reached a point with a student where tardiness made you angry, but when you learned the full story, it broke your heart?

We must remember that compliance isn't the full measure of a student. From the point of view of compliance, a student who lacks the support of an adult at home to get to school on time is a problem. Tardiness is seen as an outcome. But if, instead, that tardiness is a starting point for our empathy, we can see an opportunity to invest in improving outcomes, not just for that student's day, or school career, but for the whole school. When we pause, listen, and understand explanations rather than dismiss excuses, we may learn that there are bigger issues to deal with.

What's the Return on Rules?

In fact, most of what we give our attention to in school seems to have to do with school rules. I would argue that we put more effort into enforcing school rules than we do to the academic, creative, and social-emotional well-being of our students (and staff, for that matter). However, I think it's clear that there's a greater return on an investment in our student's well-being.

Of course, tardiness *is* a problem. But how can we address issues of attendance in a way that improves student morale? Our school culture will improve when we change our approach—especially our comments and responses—to student attendance and tardiness from one of compliance to one of investment. Consider the following suggestions for when anyone—student *or* staff—is late:

- Never make assumptions about why someone is late.
- Don't use sarcasm with someone who arrives late.
- Don't address tardiness in the moment; find out why an individual is late later in private.
- Consult others privately to discuss measures to help with underlying issues.

The way we talk to our students in the moment is pivotal for changing the culture around timeliness in our schools. Replace old responses with new language.

Instead of	Try
"Where have you been?"	"I am glad you are here."
"Where were you yesterday?"	"I missed you yesterday."
"I didn't think you were coming back."	"I am glad you are back."
"You've missed so much class."	"I was beginning to worry about you."

We know one thing for sure: what we have been doing for years isn't working. No rule, regulation, detention, consequence, punishment, or suspension is going to consistently keep kids from being late, skipping school, or missing deadlines. There is a greater potential for impact in cultivating personal, sincere, and empathetic relationships with students who face real struggles. If we do that, we can find solutions and assist our students.

When we come together as a team or as an entire staff and begin to address issues with kindness and without judgment rather than an attitude of "dealing with" students, we have better chances of influencing behavior in a positive way.

It's Not Just Kids

Let's try a thought experiment. I'd like to contemplate what would happen if we spent as much time addressing tardiness among the adults in schools as we do for students. Just for a moment, think about all of the times adults are late. Here is quick rundown. Adults can be late for:

- School
- Class
- Meetings
- Turning in evaluations
- Turning in grades
- Supervision duty
- Recess duty
- Completing surveys
- Meeting deadlines

You get the point.

Believe me, I've heard it all before. We are professional adults, and sometimes things come up that cause us to be late. So why doesn't that excuse hold water coming out of the mouth of a student? It's hypocrisy at its finest. And yet we still spend so much time and energy trying to figure out how to punish students for being late for school, class, submitting assignments, meeting deadlines, completing homework, and even dressing for PE.

Whether we are addressing promptness or trying to regulate food or drink rules in classrooms, libraries, or auditoriums, we as adults need to adhere to the same rules.

It's as though we have forgotten what it feels like to be a child, teenager, or young adult in a world that to them does not seem fair with all its dumb rules—and worse those adults who go around making a big deal out of nothing. Often, we hold our students to higher standards than we hold ourselves. As a result we come across as out of touch when we want the consequences for their violations to be enforced and ours ignored. Remember, what we model is what we get so let's be sure to model the excellence we want both students and colleagues to emulate.

Chapter Seven
INVESTING BY SELF-ASSESSMENT

A shift to an investment-based perspective changes your response patterns. When things don't turn out the way that you expected, rather than blame others, ask yourself what you might have said or done to contribute to the outcome. Instead of letting your emotions get the best of you when students don't do what they are told, you pause, regroup, and ask yourself if this is going to matter a minute, hour, day, week, month, or a year from now. In many instances it won't. You can plunge back into the fray, once again investing in students rather than struggling to get them to comply.

By examining our own behavior first we can begin to establish a routine of consistent practices that students will not only better understand, but quite frankly, appreciate. The ability to self-assess and identify areas where we need to self-regulate by changing our practices is critical to success.

Rather than expect others to change their response, let's try to understand the real issues and change our approaches. We may be pleasantly surprised by the results for both the student and you.

> # When things don't turn out the way that you expected, rather than blame others, ask yourself what you might have said or done to contribute to the outcome.

Investing in Communicating

How many times have you taken valuable class time to communicate what you believed were very clear directions for the lesson of the day only to be met immediately by hands being raised and students asking the following questions:

What are we supposed to do?

Can you repeat what you said? I didn't hear you.

Huh? I'm confused.

When I served as a classroom teacher, I received all of these responses. Each time I would become a bit more agitated, voicing my displeasure, and telling my students that they needed to listen and pay closer attention.

I would get so frustrated I'd respond with, "Ask your neighbor." Eventually, I'd even say, "I'm not repeating myself anymore. Figure it out yourself if you are not going to listen." In other words, I would blame my students rather than try and understand why they were struggling to follow my directives.

What I failed to recognize at the time was that in most cases the real issue wasn't that my students weren't listening; rather it was me who was not being clear in my communication. Worse yet, I was getting so annoyed that I used my lack of patience as a punishment rather than use my patience as a teaching tool.

If what I just described is something that you have experienced, then my hope is that I can offer a few simple thoughts to help you reframe your thinking and invest in communicating with your students in the classroom in order to help you become a more effective instructor.

Before assigning a task and delivering instructions about it, ask yourself some hard questions. Are students actually positioned to be successful at completing the task, or are they ill equipped—regardless of how clear your instructions are? Do you need to offer more support that differentiates for each child? Can you imagine any student needing more explicit instructions to complete the task than you plan to provide?

You need to critically look at the task from the eyes of a student. Invest in students by putting yourself into their perspectives and imagining completing the task before you assign and explain how to execute it.

Then when explaining the task, keep these steps in mind:

1. Be sure to have all eyes on you.
2. Never begin instruction until all side conversations have ceased.

3. Write the instructions for the task where students can view them easily.

4. Deliver instructions in chunks to avoid overwhelming your students.

5. When possible, demonstrate to the students what exactly you want them to do—modeling not only helps students better understand but gets them excited to follow your example.

When students are following your directions and completing the task, circulate and identify which students still need more clarity. Point to any visuals and have the students review them independently before asking more questions. At your discretion, you can stop the activity and review directions again and provide clarification.

Solving Problems versus Empowering Problem Solvers

Early on in my career as a teacher I wanted to solve every student problem that came my way. In fact, I thought that it is what strong educators did. I won't lie, not only did I think I could fix every problem, I *wanted* to fix every problem. It made me feel good. I was helping students, and most of the time they appreciated it.

However, what I eventually learned was that not only did the problems never go away, they seemed to multiply ten times over. I began to see my students as a burden. I was critical of them, as though somehow they were incapable of solving their own problems. Ironically, what I failed to do was to reflect and look at my own skill set.

Had I done so, I would have recognized that the real assistance I could provide to them was not rescuing them from difficult situations but accepting that it was okay to let them struggle. Rather I could support them by asking questions so that I (and they) could understand their dilemmas better. Then I could provide follow-up questions to help them come up with ideas to help them resolve their issues.

Sadly, rather than helping my students unleash their potential, I chose instead to label them and treated *them* like they were the problem. How wrong I was to model such behavior.

Please understand that I'm not blaming myself for modeling the wrong behavior. What I failed to understand early on in my tenure as a teacher was that my responsibility was to not simply to teach them as my students but support them in becoming better learners. I was never taught how to invest in my students. Sure, I was told that developing students was important, but I wasn't given the tools or processes to follow in order to truly support learning and build students' confidence.

It took me a long time to learn how to invest in my students. Here are a few things to consider when you're investing in your students becoming more independent and eventually more successful in resolving their own issues:

- See both yourself and your students as learners first.
- Don't lead with possible solutions, but rather ask questions to gain (or provide) more clarity.
- Listen to concerns with the intent to understand rather than the goal of responding.
- Provide students ongoing support, time, and resources needed for a successful resolution.
- When appropriate, bring other students into the conversation to model the importance of finding resolutions as a team.
- Value all opinions in order to help nurture an environment that encourages curiosity.

- Follow up with an encouraging word or note and then check in again to recognize and celebrate progress.

Encourage students to repeat these actions in other similar situations they encounter to support and honor their growth as learners.

For the most part, almost every dilemma you will encounter as a classroom teacher will have a solution. But you don't always have to be the one who comes up with it. Supporting students in their attempts to resolve an issue by focusing on a process to help develop their skills will prevent you from completely exhausting yourself trying to fix everything all by yourself, and it will transform the way you build relationships with students.

Chapter Eight

IS IT WORTH IT?

I think one of hardest parts about being an educator is that we often don't get to see the results of our investments immediately. Like many of you, I can recall working diligently to help a student after school to catch up on homework, coming in early so another could make up a quiz or test, and on occasion, giving up my prep or lunch time to talk to a student who was having a hard time and needed some guidance. Out of the blue you get a notice that the student has moved, and you feel devastated. You've invested so much, and then the student you believed you could help is gone. Repeat this same scenario with other students who need similar support, and next thing you know, you are starting to question whether all the work is worth it or not. Then one day you encounter a new student who requires a similar level of support and you ask yourself, "Is it really worth trying today if I don't know what will happen tomorrow?"

And just like that, the belief you once had that you could make a difference by investing your personal time, energy, and compassion in kids wavers, and you miss an opportunity to let your excellence shine!

Let me say this. When we quit on a student, they know it, and we know it. We know we didn't make a difference. Over the years there have been times when I've asked a struggling student, "How come you didn't come talk to me or another adult?" Perhaps I was asking the wrong question—or rather, the wrong person. Maybe I should have asked myself why the student decided not to come to me?

When we refuse to give up on a student, we're left with the hope and faith that maybe, just maybe, we left our mark somewhere on that student's life. When we help a student become a better version of themselves, we, in turn, become a better version of ourselves.

It's critical that we reflect on what we show our students. We have the power to make a kid walk out of class feeling better than they did before they walked in. The opposite is also true. We should never approach them with an I-will-if-you-will attitude. Rather, we should show them that we'll do our part whether they do theirs or not. This is important because kids don't just hear us—they imitate us.

> **We have the power to make a kid walk out of class feeling better than they did before they walked in.**

Reflecting on Excellence

- What's happening in your school that prevents stronger relationships between students and adults to flourish?

- Can you think of a time as a student where you struggled to remain confident in your ability to be successful? How did it make you feel? Was there someone who helped you move past this feeling? What made the difference?

- What can we do differently in our interactions with students and staff every day to make sure we build them up?

- Can you think of times when you've seen your own mind-set—of compliance or investment—reflected in a student's behavior?

PART THREE

VALUING

Colleagues

TO LOVE OURSELVES AND SUPPORT EACH OTHER IN
THE PROCESS OF BECOMING REAL IS PERHAPS THE
GREATEST SINGLE ACT OF DARING GREATLY.
—BRENÉ BROWN

Chapter Nine
THE INFLUENCE OF INVESTMENT

I will spare you the details of how I lost my way and simply tell you that I became a two-time dropout after struggling with the rigors of college. So at the age of nineteen, my parents finally agreed to let me do what I always wanted to do: work.

I arrived at the job fair at the Comfort Inn an hour early, full of energy, and ready to make my parents proud of me. Soon, a gentleman came up to me and shook my hand and introduced himself as Bob. "Lombardi time, huh? That is a great first impression young man." (For anyone unfamiliar with legendary football coach Vince Lombardi, he famously considered his players late if they didn't arrive fifteen minutes *early* for practice.)

For the next hour, I was asked all sorts of questions, mainly about my willingness to work long stretches away from home and family. Bob and his partner asked me if I had a car, and they wanted to know if I would be willing to talk to people that I had never met before. Never once did they tell me what their business was or the name of their company. But I could tell Bob liked me. When the interview was over, Bob asked me to wait outside.

Within a few minutes, he came out and asked me to join him and two other gentlemen that were not in the first interview. He indicated that he liked my disposition. He said I had charm and charisma and a natural smile that others would find appealing. Then, without warning, he asked, "Why should we hire you?"

"Because I am willing to take the job even though I still don't even know what it is I would be doing," I responded.

Bob smiled, looked at the other two men and said, "I like this kid. Randy, you can take him for your region. Someday, we all may be working for him." Needless to say, I walked out of there with the biggest smile on my face. I was on my way.

Within six months, I was the top-selling health insurance agent in the Midwest region. Life was good, but most importantly, my mom and dad were proud of me.

I often worked alongside Randy, my regional manager. He was almost fifty years of age with a wife and three children. Randy was like a father figure to me, always mentoring me and encouraging me to return to school someday. His comments were sincere, and his approach was genuine. He always seemed to have my best interest at heart. I enjoyed the meaningful conversations we'd have. "Jim," he would say (he always called me Jim), "don't ever think that you can't go back to school. I guarantee you one thing. You will never look back on your life and say, 'What was I thinking? I can't believe I got a college diploma.'" He talked often of how he had spent twenty-five years on the road trying to make a living for his family. He would talk about how he wished he had gone to college, but his time had come and gone. Besides, he was making good money now. By all accounts, he was successful and had positioned himself well within the company. But I could tell that he missed spending time with his children.

He was also different from the others I worked with in one way. While the other salespeople and managers were friendly, they were also reluctant to share their experiences and their craft with me.

Knowing we would be eventually compete with one another for sales, they weren't especially eager to share their recipe for success. Not Randy. Every opportunity he had, he invested time in me. He often shared little tips about how to close a sale. Other times he would ask me to ride along with him just so he could share his insights and what he had learned over the years on the road.

At the time I heard Randy's words but didn't really absorb them. After all, I was enjoying my work, and I was good at it as well. So good in fact that less than a year later I cost Randy his job. Randy and I were working in Missouri when the news came down. I returned from the field after a successful day to find that Bob wanted to meet with me. We walked outside, and he began to talk about the day he hired me.

"You know, son, I knew you were going to be something special the day I met you. I spoke to the president this morning, and I told him that we needed to promote you to regional manager. Of course, this will include a $25,000 salary plus benefits and commission. With your team under you, you can easily earn six figures. Congratulations! You can call your parents and tell them that you have made it."

I was stunned. I thought back to the times I'd spent sitting on the couch next to my parents crying, wanting to quit school, so uncertain about my future. Now, at nineteen, I had made my mark.

The next day, Randy and I headed back to Iowa. He didn't say much in the car. I knew that things would never be the same between him and I. How could they? I was nineteen and had taken away his livelihood. He was almost fifty, with a wife and three kids to support. I dropped him off at home that afternoon. I wasn't sure what to say to him, so I said the only thing I could, "Thanks for everything, Randy."

When I walked into the house, my parents were there to give me the biggest hug. I cried, but I wasn't sure if it was because I felt their pride or because Randy had been fired. I was heartbroken.

My mentor, my friend, my partner—gone. That night Bob called and asked to meet with me the next morning to talk about my new responsibilities. We arranged to meet in Cedar Rapids.

On the way to meet him the next day, I couldn't stop thinking about Randy. Was that how I would end up someday? Would I give my life to a company and have it all taken away in one night? Spend my career on the road away from my family and then not be able to support them because the company decided I was no longer making enough money for them? He had invested so much time helping me be successful. And what about his advice about going back to school? He really cared about me. He believed in me. By investing in me, he had shown me what it meant to live your excellence.

I can't remember much of my conversation that day with Bob. That's probably because I had so many other things on my mind. I'm sure I told him I was grateful for the promotion and for taking a chance on me. I do remember that he became angry when I told him I was thinking about returning to school and was hoping he would allow me to work part time. I think he realized he had under-estimated how much my relationship with Randy mattered to me. He became furious as he asked, "After everything I've done for you, you're just going to throw it all away over school?"

In that moment, I realized that if Bob really cared about me, he would have encouraged me to return to school to get my education just like Randy had done almost every day. Instead, he was upset that I wasn't complying with his vision and his needs.

In the end I took Randy's advice and went back to school full time. His investment in me made a world of difference. It paid off, even though he wasn't there to see it. In the same way, I believe you can have a huge influence not just on students but on colleagues as well when you invest in them. The same way Randy saw value in me, you see their value.

Chapter Ten

EVERY CONTRIBUTION, EVERY DAY

Each one of us is responsible for our own morale. We cannot and should not allow others to live rent free in our heads. Having said that, I know that all of us from time to time fall victim to allowing others to dictate our moods and our attitudes. No one is immune.

There have been times throughout my career when I allowed the words, actions, or behaviors of others to determine how I approached my day. I was most susceptible when I was tired, frustrated, or feeling like my work wasn't valued. There were times when I felt my supervisors didn't appreciate my sacrifices—like the time I spent away from family. Maybe some of you have experienced that feeling.

But if I'm being honest, I must admit that I've been on the other end of situations like this. I know I've negatively affected colleagues as a result of my actions. I didn't do so intentionally, but the simple fact is that we all experience moments where we fall short. Let these moments serve as reminders that, regardless of what our titles in our schools might be, all of us play a role in determining the morale of those we work alongside.

I still feel strongly that ultimately we are responsible for our own attitudes and the level of energy we bring to the table each day, but I also know that we can impact and influence others merely by the way we treat them.

Investing by Validating

A recent conversation with a principal reminded me of the power we can have to make a positive effect on the morale of those around us by how we respond to their ideas and suggestions.

This principal had reached out to a director at his central office regarding a concern that he and others had. He didn't only point out the problem; he offered to help by sharing a possible solution and some resources. The response from the director was dismissive. It seemed like he didn't see the problem, and he wasn't interested in the resources the principal had offered. What made matters worse, was that the director later did a complete one-eighty after hearing about the same issue from some others in the district. Eventually, at the director's behest, the district moved forward with the solution the principal had initially suggested—but with no acknowledgment of the principal's contribution. The principal was left feeling underappreciated and unseen by his district.

Actions like the director's aren't always ill intentioned. There will be always moments when our interactions leave others feeling slighted, but if we recognize that we can make a positive impact when we are intentional in acknowledging and validating the contributions of others, we minimize the chances of leaving our staff feeling empty and underappreciated. When we dismiss or fail to acknowledge the contributions—regardless of how big or small—of students and staff, we miss an opportunity to strengthen the core of our community and to value what people bring to the organization.

What can you do to acknowledge and validate the suggestions of others while strengthening morale? Create a structured process for handling concerns, calls, and complaints so everyone is on the same page, one that's rooted in communication.

Immediately upon receiving a suggestion from a student or coworker, thank them for investing the time to share their thoughts and ideas with you. Then be sure to follow up with a real conversation (face to face or on the phone) so that you can learn what they've already done to help move an idea forward and gauge their level of concern. Before you're done, let them know that you plan to reach out to others to get their perspectives and that you will get back to them.

Once you have collected more information on the issue, bring all parties together. Start by thanking them for their input, and share your thoughts on how you plan to handle the matter moving forward. Gather feedback again before making a final decision. Let everyone know the decision-making process you used, who was involved, and

When we dismiss or fail to acknowledge the contributions–regardless of how big or small–of students and staff, we miss an opportunity to strengthen the core of our community and to value what people bring to the organization.

the reasons behind your decision in order to provide clarity and reduce confusion. Follow up with the individual who first brought the issue to your attention, and thank them for their time and more importantly for their leadership.

We cultivate trust when we take the time to personally invest our time in others, and we build confidence when we listen to them and validate their ideas not only by our words but especially through our actions. That's what a culture of investment looks and feels like from the inside.

The Problem with Rock Stars

There will always be times when we just need to rescue ourselves from . . . well, ourselves. I cannot even begin to tell you how many times I've shared something with my staff thinking I was spot on in my message but didn't realize what I was sharing was actually dividing my colleagues with my words and actions. Although this was never my intent, my actions created dissent rather than community.

This comes back to compliance versus investment—even when you think you're making a positive statement. The compliance mindset views praise as a reward, something that people in an organization want from a leader, end of story. But a leader with an investment mindset understands that any action—be it praise or punishment—must be considered from the perspectives of everyone involved: the principal giving praise, the educator receiving it, and even the other educators in the school. That's because leading from an investment perspective means not only identifying the value in the others around you but working with them together to create a culture based on that value.

If we want to create a culture of investment in our teams, staffs, and schools, we need to recognize the contributions of everyone involved in our work—without letting our words or behaviors create resentments that eventually lead to a culture of compliance.

On one occasion I found myself needing to be rescued during a staff meeting where I had introduced some new staff members. In my excitement of wanting to lavish them with praise, I referred to them as "rock stars."

Only later, did I learn how my words had been taken by some of the veteran staff. I also realized the unintended pressures and scrutiny I had placed on these new teachers by referring to them in such a way. Some staff members shared with me privately how this "rock star" label, although meant as a sincere compliment, had a detrimental effect on them because it created a sense of resentment from some of their colleagues who felt slighted because they had never received such high praise, even after having served in the building for years. They shared how my comments were followed by jealousy and digs made about them by others. At one moment they were being recognized for their skills, excellent performance, and successful outcomes by their supervisor, and then in the next moment, they felt ostracized by their own peers.

I've had private conversations with teachers and administrators who were recipients of awards who told me about their personal experiences of having been recognized. On the one hand they felt an immense sense of pride, and yet they felt serious consternation due to the negative response shown to them by some of their colleagues. They were meant to have felt lifted up. Instead, they felt a cloud of shame and guilt over them because their peers thought their award-winning efforts to bring their best to their students and schools made everyone else look bad.

Here are a few comments that have been shared with me on this topic from folks I want to thank for pushing my thinking. Each of them makes me want to continue to want to be better for others, for you, and for myself as well.

Sometimes the investment made by "rock star teachers" isn't realistic or sustainable for the vast majority of teachers.

—Bill Ferriter, @plugusin

On the other hand, being that teacher that is a "rock star" can be very stressful. I feel like I am constantly being scrutinized and I wonder what will happen when/if I don't meet the expectations for me. We need to find a balance.

—MadnessInTheMiddle, @twhite1489

I believe we all have the potential for rock star moments, not necessarily a rock star career. Spotlight the positives when they happen, but always look for those whose shining moments others might overlook.

—Tamara Letter, @tamaraletter

I now see that labeling some staff members as rock stars can work against us, especially if we aim to cultivate a culture where everyone in the organization feels appreciated. When you point to one person as a "rock star teacher," the other teachers understand that they're not as highly valued—whether that's what you meant or not. The same can be said of other labels for teachers like "superstar," "master," or "model."

It's not that we shouldn't lift up new or outstanding members of our teaching community. Rather, if we are truly invested in educational excellence, we should expect a high level of performance across the board from all teachers. What message do we send when our expectations are not consistent, when what we expect of one staff member is not the same as what we expect of another?

If we are interested in creating and maintaining high teaching and coaching standards, then the question is how to get there. We can simply demand that everyone comply with the standard we've set—but you can guess how that would work out. Or we can devise and put in place support systems for everyone to receive high-quality coaching, guidance, and resources as well as the time needed to improve, not only for the kids they teach and their colleagues but for themselves.

If we provide such support while acknowledging that no one is anywhere near perfect, I think it is not only reasonable but likely that all staff members will strive for rock star status every day.

When we all intentionally lift each other up, we build a sense of community among the staff where we all can be celebrated and honored for striving to do what we expect kids to do every day: our very best. Isn't that what we want of everyone? Whatever your best is on any given day, bring it to the classroom, school offices, library, stage, or athletic fields.

Praising Forward

Of course, there are times when it's best to praise a contribution. I remember having a conversation with a principal whose school was considered by all measures one of the best in the state of Wisconsin at that time. He shared that he never apologized for having great programs, but he worked to change the whole system by creating an environment where every program wanted to be the best for each other. This combination of pride and community is a model for inspiring greatness in all of our programs.

We often don't give enough of our time and energy to those individuals in our organizations who are doing all that we ask of them. But instead of singling one person's success at the expense of another, what better compliment is there than allowing them to carry the banner of their great work forward?

We can strive for excellence without leaving anyone behind by not thinking of greatness as an end result—that old compliance trap where something is either great or not—but rather as the beginning of more greatness. By understanding and modeling the processes a program has followed to achieve success, we can find an incredible opportunity to invest in further efforts.

So how can we elevate all of our efforts to greatness without apologizing for success?

- Encourage all members of your organization to strive for greatness, and provide the necessary support so they can achieve it.
- Don't just tell others that you expect them to build great programs but provide the opportunity to envision them together.
- Allow the educators you work with to learn from those who have already built great programs and help them understand not only their strategies and practices but the thought processes behind their decisions.
- Make sure to give individuals and programs the TLC needed to continue to sustain their greatness over time. Even the greatest of programs can fall back to average.
- Be sure to visit and attend your school's programs and events and ask questions of your staff. Your investment of time and efforts to understand what's happening show that you value your staff.

All programs—whether they're great already or on the way—have people who want to be recognized for their work. Make sure every teacher, librarian, director, principal, counselor, coach, activity sponsor, social worker, and nurse always feels respected and supported and—most importantly—that you are invested in their program's success. There's no better praise than investment, and no better way to show that you're invested than by attending, supporting, cheering for, and recognizing all students and staff with the same level of pride and intensity for all academic, athletic, special needs, electives, career, technical, and fine arts programs.

Chapter Eleven
WHEN EDUCATORS GOSSIP

Nothing hurts like unkind chatter at work among colleagues. Often personal details are shared with the intention of causing personal harm and damage to someone's reputation. These comments, regardless of whether they are false, true, or somewhere in between, are toxic to schools, businesses, and organizations alike.

Until we begin to address the gossip in our workplace, we will never reach the standard of excellence most educational organizations aspire to achieve or—in most cases—expect and even advertise. Over the years, I have encountered countless educators who have been victims of hateful gossip. Others have successfully avoided becoming targets but have shared with me privately that they are at a loss for what to do when it comes to dealing with the gossipers in their schools. When they describe the level of toxicity in their organizations and share examples of the things that are said, I can't help but think that the amount of gossiping that exists in our schools and organizations has reached epidemic proportions.

Our teachers and support staff cannot be at their best if they are worrying about finding themselves at the mercy of hurtful

> **Until we begin to address the gossip in our workplace, we will never reach the standard of excellence most educational organizations aspire to achieve.**

gossip. Many of the individuals with whom I have spoken were genuinely hurting, struggling about how to respond, and even contemplating leaving their schools in hopes of finding a healthier culture. They had grown tired and weary of seeing the negative impact on their teammates. This is discouraging on so many levels because, quite frankly, we cannot afford to be losing dedicated and caring school employees to boorish behavior.

We know that when we gossip, it actually says more about us than the people we are gossiping about. Classroom educators intervene to stop students from gossiping. So why do we stay silent when it involves adults? Perhaps it's because we don't know what to do. How can we use an investment mindset to care for and support teachers and staff so they can avoid or minimize the potential for gossip in many of our schools today?

Here are some suggestions on how to address the gossipers in our organizations whose behaviors tear at the seams of a culture of investment.

1. Take time to listen to what a gossiper has to say, but prepare yourself to respond. Staying silent could give the impression that you agree with their comments.

2. Follow up with questions. Make sure that you haven't misunderstood what was shared while at the same time being clear that you are not taking sides.

3. Let those who gossip to you directly know that you appreciate the fact they felt comfortable enough to share such comments with you. However, be sure to not come across as party to the gossip.

4. Defend the victim. Respond to the gossiper by telling them that their story does not reflect your personal experience and, regardless, it is not your place to judge.

5. Remind the gossiper that we are all vulnerable to others sharing things about us that are hurtful.

6. Challenge the gossiper in a respectful way. Ask if they have had an opportunity to communicate with the person they are gossiping about.

7. Advocate for the victim by pointing out to the gossiper that most people, if given the opportunity, would want to be given the opportunity to respond before comments are shared about them.

8. Promise the gossiper that they need not worry that you will not share what they've said with others, especially the intended target.

9. Encourage them again to go talk to the individual they are talking to you about. Make it clear you have no desire to listen to their comments again until they have shared their thoughts openly with the person they were talking about.

10. Give them permission to come talk to you again to share what they learned from the other person after they have spoken to them.

11. Then walk away.

12. Maintain your integrity and never repeat to others what was shared with you.

There is no guarantee that we can eliminate gossip from the work environment forever. However, I do believe that we can reduce its toxic impact if we begin to treat the hosts in a way that reminds them that we are all prone to this disease. The only way to minimize the number of gossipers in our organizations is to take personal responsibility for combatting them with integrity. Model an investment outlook to them that shows how, as educators, we can all manage ourselves in a more caring, positive, and productive way.

Chapter Twelve

RESULTS

Investing So Others Get Results

J ust like I wanted to solve my students' problems as a teacher, as a principal, I equally saw it as my duty to solve my colleagues' problems. And just like with my students, I truly thought it was my job as an educator to do so.

It won't come as a surprise to discover that, just as they had with my students, the problems I was solving would proliferate. I started to view my colleagues as weak and, just like my students, incapable of solving their own problems. And again the problem was with me. If I had invested in my colleagues and helped build their capacity for solving problems, almost all of the problems that I encountered would be resolved without me having to play a leading role.

If you have an investment-based mindset, you understand that supporting others doesn't mean solving their problems but rather asking questions to understand their dilemmas better and then providing follow-up questions to help them come up with ideas to these issues.

I became motivated when I finally recognized and accepted the issues with my problem-solving tendencies. I was determined to work harder at being intentional with those around me by spending more time in conversation in order to create an investment-based culture in my school. It all fell into place for me one day when I was interviewing one of our paraprofessional educators.

I asked her, "If you became the principal today, what is one change you would make and why?" I still remember her hesitation. I was sure she was having a hard time answering because she didn't want to say anything critical of my performance as principal. "It's okay, you can tell me. I won't take it personally," I said. "I asked the question because I really want to know and I need your help in order to get better."

She looked at me and responded, "OK, well a few of us have been talking. Do you think it would be possible to find a place for us to put our coats and purses?"

Wow. Here I had been the principal for five years at this school and never once had it crossed my mind that this was an issue. It made perfect sense of course. Our aides didn't have a classroom, office, or closet to store their personal belongings in. Sitting down and asking this staff member a few questions had not only generated a whole new perspective for me, it also created a pathway to a new way of approaching school culture.

For the next few years we, as an administrative team and with support from our office staff, began investing in one another by exchanging two of our most precious commodities: the gift of time and the gift of love. What we learned was that we had not been taught a process for how to listen and learn from one another to create an investment-based culture.

What I said earlier about empowering students applies with equal force when working with colleagues:

- See both yourself and your fellow educators as learners first.
- Don't lead with possible solutions, but rather ask questions to gain (or provide) more clarity.
- Listen to concerns with the intent to understand rather than the goal of responding.
- Provide staff ongoing support, time, and resources needed for a successful resolution.
- When appropriate, bring other colleagues into the conversation to model the importance of finding resolutions as a team.
- Value all opinions in order to help nurture an environment that encourages curiosity.
- When colleagues struggle to resolve their own issues, don't stamp them with a label.
- Ask staff if they are willing to invest in the process and partner with you to resolve the issue or concern.

Encourage colleagues to repeat these actions in other similar situations they encounter to support and honor their growth as learners.

And what's true of the classroom is also true of administration: almost every dilemma you will encounter as an educator will have a solution. It just doesn't have to be you who comes up with it. Supporting colleagues in their quests to resolve issues by focusing on a process to help develop their skills will go a long way in building your relationships with them. It will also keep your desk clear of the little issues, allowing you to concentrate on the bigger ones. Most importantly, building this capacity in your colleagues is essential if you want to instill an investment-based outlook in your school.

Getting the Results You Want

Have you ever walked away from an interaction frustrated because the outcomes you were hoping to see never materialized? Have you ever been disappointed in a colleague or staff member because they had not completed a task or project in the way you had expected them to?

If you are like me, this has happened to you more than once in your time as an educational leader. If it continues to happen, then it might be time to address your frustrations by examining your own practices.

There certainly have been times when I've realized I needed to manage my approach differently to achieve the results I was hoping to get. I recall feeling so frustrated in one particular situation that I finally reached out to a mentor of mine I greatly respect and asked him for some advice because I was at a loss for what to do. Although he is not an educator, this mentor is a successful businessman who was able to offer me some advice on how to move forward. I will never forget the words that he spoke to me that day: "Managing

There certainly have been times when I've realized I needed to manage my approach differently to achieve the results I was hoping to get.

people to achieve the results we want requires of us a clear process for achieving those results."

That struck a chord with me, and I began to reflect on my own practices as a school principal. What were my processes? What was I bringing to the table?

I think a lot about what it takes to bring about change such that school cultures become investment based, and I've determined that more often than not success is determined by the processes we adopt. Here are the steps I take to ensure that I'm thinking about investing in others:

1. **Determine the outcome you want.** Often, we are not clear what it is we want to accomplish. Our own inability to conceive of this vision can set us up for failure before we ever begin.

2. **Establish clear expectations.** We must be clear in communicating exactly what it is we want. It is extremely difficult for colleagues to demonstrate their competence when we are vague in our requests. Remember that clarity precedes competence.

3. **Provide examples.** Describing and/or showing the goal we hope to accomplish is necessary in order for others to understand the standard of excellence we aim to achieve.

4. **Give opportunities for questions.** Be sure to provide ample time for questions and dialogue to enable people to process the information you give them. No one can invest in what they don't understand.

5. **Review expectations.** After responding to questions, be sure to go over your expectations one more time. Don't assume that because you communicated your expectations once that the information was processed correctly.

6. **Model the standard you want others to achieve.** Before we can expect others to perform at a high standard, we need to make sure our performance is at an equal standard.

7. **Send off with confidence.** Following the steps above will help reduce the anxiety felt by colleagues when given a new task to accomplish. Remember, it is our responsibility to instill a sense of confidence in others through our words and actions.

8. **Initiate progress checks.** Create a schedule to follow up in order to see how things are developing. We know the calendar of our colleagues can be extremely hectic at times, so initiate these important follow-ups in order to stay focused and maintain the agreed-upon timeline. By waiting until the end to check on things, you are putting a successful outcome at risk.

9. **Offer support and coaching.** Checking in on a regular basis also allows you to ensure colleagues are receiving the support they need. The more time you spend observing their work the more genuine and effective coaching conversations will be.

10. **Show gratitude.** Be grateful for the educators you work with. Appreciate others and the value they bring to the organization, regardless of their roles.

11. **Extend honest feedback.** If a colleague doesn't meet the expectations you've set, they deserve honest feedback that is delivered in a caring and compassionate manner, an opportunity to respond to your feedback, and the experience of working in an environment that truly supports coaching people to not only expect their best but to be their best.

As you continue on your journey as an educator, I encourage you to revisit your processes for achieving the results you aspire to achieve. Implement them in a consistent and fair way with the goal of growing and developing an investment mindset in all your colleagues, recognizing the different skills they bring to the table.

Chapter Thirteen
SUSTAINING AN INVESTMENT OUTLOOK

We don't always get it right. But if we are able to recognize that we will make mistakes and then apologize for our missteps with sincerity, then I think we stand a good chance of getting a pass when we don't meet others' expectations.

Almost every staff member that I have met, regardless of their position, approaches each day with one goal in mind: to bring their best and give their best to others in order to ensure that every student and every staff member experiences success and feels a sense of belonging. Bus drivers, kitchen staff, school nurses, paras, tech staff, custodians, secretaries, instructional coaches, and curriculum directors all keep their eyes on the prize along with the teachers and administrators in order to help every member of the school community reach this feeling. They accept there will be challenges along the way, especially when the stresses of the job cause us to lose our focus and stray away from the things we know matter.

Here are eight reminders to help you maintain your focus throughout the school year and keep your *I*'s on an investment outlook.

> **When you start to feel like the work you do no longer matters, keep going. You will eventually see that it does matter to someone—even if you don't recognize it at that moment.**

- **Invest** in your students and colleagues every day. Engage them, spend time with them, listen to them, believe in them, encourage them, support them, trust them, and—when they mess up—forgive them. Give them your most precious commodity, the gift of time.
- **Influence** their beliefs and their behaviors. Model what you expect, shape their thinking, develop their skill sets, speak the truth, and leverage their strengths. Invite them to lead others, and more importantly, allow them to determine their own pathways in order to build capacity.
- **Inspire** their work. Ignite their passion, awaken their dreams, rekindle their hope, energize their spirit, and prompt them when needed. Give them permission to create and innovate without fear of judgement or negative evaluation.
- **Invite** their input. Ask them what they think, what they believe, and most importantly, why they believe what they believe. This will allow you to really get to understand their

core beliefs and what drives their behavior so you can support their work with integrity and without hesitation.

- **Initiate** the work that needs to be done. It begins with you. If you are feeling overwhelmed, pick one item or area and just begin. Invite others in. Get started today! When you start to feel like the work you do no longer matters, keep going. You will eventually see that it does matter to someone—even if you don't recognize it at that moment.

- **Improve** the work environment. Redefine your expectations. Raise the standards. Enhance the workplace by bringing in evidence of student learning to remind everyone of why we do the work that we do. Exceed your own expectations by helping others exceed theirs.

- **Inform** your team by communicating effectively. Respond promptly when contacted. Keep students and staff apprised of ongoing matters. Notify your superiors of potential conflicts. Advise others only when asked. Don't tell others what they want to hear; tell them what you really believe in a kind and caring way. Don't ignore or avoid obvious wrongdoings for fear of confrontation. Remember, the best form of communication is still face to face because it gives us the opportunity to cultivate stronger relationships.

- **Impact** students and staff by bringing meaning to their work. Don't ask others to do what you are not willing to do yourself. View them by the significance of their work and their impact on others, especially kids. Take time to show your appreciation—in writing or verbally—for something that is personal to them or that demonstrates their effect on others. Everyone wants to be memorable. Do your part to leave a lasting impression.

Working in a school can sometimes feel like you are in a sprint every day. It can leave you feeling exhausted and overwhelmed.

When it comes to our work, it is our responsibility to show others that we are learners first in this journey every day.

Reflecting on Excellence

- You hear colleagues begin to complain about a teacher. You don't want to become a silent participant, but you also don't want to alienate your peers. How do you respond?

- "If educators are always asking for permission, you haven't done a very good job of building capacity." What does this mean to you? How do you handle educators that frequently ask questions or come to you for support? Imagine a conversation that would minimize the time they would need from others while at the same time developing their leadership skills and confidence.

- What are the things that make you personally feel valued? In what ways do you show appreciation for your students and staff? How can you make every student and every staff member in your school feel valued and appreciated?

PART FOUR

DEVELOPING

Leadership

WE DEFINE OURSELVES BY THE BEST
THAT IS IN US, NOT BY THE WORST
THAT HAS BEEN DONE TO US.

—EDWARD LEWIS

Chapter Fourteen
THE COURAGE TO ACT AND
THE COURAGE TO ASK

I still recall one day during my first year as principal when a student walked into the main office asking to see me because he was genuinely concerned that his music teacher had passed away in the classroom. He told me that the teacher was not responsive to the student's calls or taps on the shoulder as they attempted to rouse her.

You can imagine the horror and urgency I felt as I quickly made my way to the classroom.

Fortunately, the teacher had not passed away. She was alert and talking to the students when I entered the classroom, though I later learned she had slept through the end of one class and into the beginning of the next.

Admittedly, the frightened student's report was not the first time I had heard rumors about this teacher. In fact, it was pretty well-known by students and staff that she would fall asleep during class on a daily basis. You may be asking yourself at this point that if this was common knowledge, then why had it not been addressed, especially when it could affect the safety and well-being of the students in the teacher's class.

Here's the truth: I had no idea even how to begin the conversation. I was embarrassed for her and reluctant to even bring up the issue for fear of upsetting her. I had heard the whispers of others who had confronted her about it previously only to quickly suffer her wrath and verbal abuse. Moreover, I was concerned that a misstep in handling this issue would create a school-wide problem for me starting with creating a strain on the relationship between myself and this staff member. It could lead to either (or both) the perception among the staff that I didn't support my teachers or gossip that I didn't respond to complaints brought by students and parents.

I was in over my head as a rookie principal, struggling to survive as I tried to navigate the sometimes treacherous waters of school leadership. But the challenges of working with teachers who aren't fulfilling basic expectations isn't something exclusive to rookie administrators. A few years ago I received an email from a principal who had attended a workshop that I had conducted for school leaders and aspiring administrators. He shared with me that he was struggling with a couple of teachers who weren't fulfilling responsibilities he'd given them regarding phone calls home for students who were in the D–F range. After reading through his email I asked him to give me a call so I could better advise him.

However, I was somewhat caught off guard when after sharing this story with the principal he said, "Jimmy, this is my eighth year as a principal and after hearing you speak, I realized I need to get better in this area." I have to admit that I felt bad for him. *Eight years* into his tenure as principal and he was sharing with me that he didn't know how to approach this issue with his staff. I couldn't help but think how many other principals were lying awake at night having these same feelings and struggling to come up with the best way to address similar situations.

The Five *W*'s of Leadership

Who you are as a leader should be the same person you are as a person. Know your core, share your core, and then live your core.

What challenges you face on a daily basis do not need to define you. But how you respond to them will determine your character.

When you are feeling disappointed and find yourself falling to average, remember that your personal excellence starts over again tomorrow.

Where some complain and place blame on others, recognize that you are responsible for your own feelings and it's your choice whether those experiences leave you energized or depleted.

Why some students and educators lose their passion for learning and teaching we may never know, but never stop believing that you can inspire them back to greatness.

We don't need to put so much pressure on ourselves by pretending we have it all figured out. A sincere and genuine approach can go a long way in addressing concerns or issues. Over the years I have learned that most students and staff will respect and appreciate us more when we keep difficult conversations real and recognize our shortcomings, rather than pretend we have all of the answers.

Begin Where You Are

I believe that many of the issues that we face in schools today are actually (and unintentionally) created by us, the building and district leaders. I don't expect everyone to agree with me on this point, (especially building and district leaders). After all, who wants to admit that they are the problem?

Well, I will. And I didn't know it at the time. Quite frankly, my experiences have led me to believe that others, like me, also don't see it. Those who do see and are aware of the problems they're causing are often not sure what to do about it.

Then there are those who have come to the realization that they are in over their heads but are afraid to admit it—because admitting it means admitting having failed. For many of us who went into leadership roles, that's a hard pill to swallow. Think about it. How many principals do you think have actually walked into their superintendent's office and told their boss, "I don't know what the hell I'm doing." My guess is not too many.

There are days when principals don't know what to do. They hesitate. They want to do the right thing not only for the students but for staff too. But sometimes they don't know what the right thing is. Or maybe they do know, but they hesitate, unsure if it's worth the time and amount of work it may require of them. They worry because they don't want their staff to not feel supported. Sometimes they feel bad because they can see how tired everyone is. But they don't know how to make each person feel better. And there are moments when they fall short of expectations or do or say the wrong thing.

It's true. Principals are far from perfect. They went into this role believing they were ready for the challenges that lay ahead of them, but it's impossible to truly understand the complexities of the job and the emotional toll these challenges can take until you're in it. I feel their frustrations and understand their deficiencies and I appreciate them because I lived them. I wanted to be great for my staff, for our students, our parents, and my own family, and I also know there were times I let them down.

Let's try and give ourselves a little relief by remembering that we make more moment-to-moment decisions than most. Because of that it's inevitable that we will unintentionally make errors. However, we must be careful to not allow this to produce a kind of tentative thinking on our part, which could cause us to hesitate, overthink, and not trust our responses.

What's in You?

How can you begin to combat feelings of inadequacy? Begin by reminding yourself that you, like all of us, are a work in progress. We all have our good days, bad days, proud moments, and not-so-proud moments.

The next thing we can do is commit to being just a little better each day! A better friend, a better colleague, a better parent, a better spouse, and yes, a better teacher and school leader. This has to begin through personal reflection and a reduction in tentative thinking. Recognize and appreciate the struggle. People who embrace their struggles seem more at peace and much more fulfilled.

I once read something that continues to help me reframe my thinking toward an investment mindset as an education leader:

> The moment you become more convinced about what's in
> you than you are afraid of what's against you, you'll begin to
> push the limits of what's possible for your life.

That part of knowing what's in you is critical—that's a sense of purpose. I think we need purpose more than we need happiness when we are struggling. Most people I know are trying to find what makes them happy, but deeply fulfilled people seem to know their purpose in life. I think that's because when you know your purpose, you never stop being yourself. That gives you the strength to face your struggles.

Take my friend Jason. I met Jason when I moved to Chicago. He served as the doorman at the condominium complex where I lived. Every day as I left or entered my building, Jason was there to greet me with a warm smile and a handshake, and more importantly, he always called me by my name. He didn't just know my name; he knew everyone's name. Jason has this incredible ability to connect with people. He has a genuine persona that others find appealing. I know this because I have stood by and observed him with admiration as he engaged person after person in conversation and asked about a family member by name or ran to open up a door or carry sacks of groceries in for a tenant.

When I see others invest their time in something that brings them joy, it's clear to me that they have figured out their sense of purpose. That something for Jason was engaging others in conversation and bringing joy to their day, especially when their mood was sour.

Jason is great at dealing with unhappy people, but, admittedly, that is one area of school life where I struggled early on in my tenure as principal: with people who complained. Let's face it, most of us don't enjoy dealing with complaints. Why? Because they suck the life out of us. So if you find yourself tired of dealing with students or staff who come across as needy or complaining or even avoiding them altogether, maybe it's time to try a different approach. You just might become a better listener along the way.

When I changed my mindset and approached complainers from an investment perspective, I was able to identify some simple steps I could take to behave my way to a better result.

1. **Listen.** Sounds simple, right? In my experience I've found that most people think they are good listeners, but our behavior indicates otherwise. How many times have we tried to listen to others only to find ourselves interrupting them midsentence? How about trying to "multitask" while someone was talking to you? Ever interjected an idea before they finished a thought? In my case? Guilty, guilty, and guilty. Try this: focus on a person's every word, maintain good eye contact, and do not give your attention to any other tasks while someone is talking to you.

2. **Ask a follow-up question.** This sends a strong message that you are interested in what someone has to say. Everyone wants to feel validated when they share a thought, idea, or concern.

3. **Summarize what they communicate.** You won't be able to summarize what the person has shared unless you are completely invested in what they are communicating. Repeating what you have just heard will earn you instant credibility and allow others to truly see you as a good listener. If you need to, take notes to help you frame their thoughts, but maintain eye contact throughout. When you summarize, you personalize.

4. **Ask what they are willing to invest.** This final question is the most crucial step in helping others recognize their own talents and empowering them to not only see themselves as problem solvers but solution makers. Asking others what they are willing to invest to help you solve their concern

gives them permission to lead and, more importantly, it keeps you from feeling depleted.

We become healthier and more effective in leading our classrooms, buildings, and districts by performing our duties as educators at a high level without expending ourselves to the point of exhaustion. When we give others permission, whether we are talking about our students, support staff, or colleagues, and invite them to lead with us, we cultivate a community where everyone sees themselves as leaders. What a tremendous feeling it is to help others build their confidence so they can feel capable of being more and doing more than they ever thought possible.

Chapter Fifteen

WHAT IT TAKES TO LEAD

I believe that everyone in an organization is a leader. Every one of us has the capacity to lead—though whether or not we choose to lead is a different issue. I would argue that on any given day, you are leading in some capacity. You lead when you make a decision, when you initiate a discussion or contribute to a conversation, and when you go out of your way to help a student or assist a colleague. Leading doesn't have to mean that you gather a group of individuals, give them a good pep talk, and inspire them to be more and do more than they ever thought possible.

So then why do so many of us still not see ourselves as leaders? And why aren't more people seeking leadership positions? What are we afraid of? Maybe we are afraid that if we say or do the wrong thing that we will be criticized, or we're worried that others will judge us harshly. Sometimes it seems that our experiences have taught us that leading makes us vulnerable to failure. We hesitate because we know how harshly those who are not able to live up to the standard of what it means to be an effective leader are treated.

Ask anyone what characteristics an effective or successful leader has and you are bound to get a multitude of responses that likely include the following:

- Servant leadership
- Courage
- A sense of humor
- Passion
- Caring
- Assertiveness
- Vision
- Communicativeness
- Empathy
- Trustworthiness
- Honesty
- Charisma
- The ability to inspire
- Confidence
- A willingness to delegate

Attributes like these are needed in order to successfully lead. But I think the way many of us view them explains why so many refuse to see themselves as leaders.

Some say that these leadership characteristics are a part of our makeup, our DNA—that some people are just born passionate or charismatic. Then, they go on to say things like, "I am just not that way. It's not who I am." Others say that traits like trustworthiness, honesty, and empathy are learned, so those who lack the role models to teach them these values never acquire them. But it's clear that many of these characteristics are really skills that must be learned over time: things like assertiveness, the willingness to delegate, and vision require a great deal of effort to master. They must be developed at a high level in order to lead effectively. You've got to put in the effort.

Is that the reason why so many of us hesitate to become leaders? In order to be an effective leader we have to be willing to examine our characteristics and ask ourselves, "Am I willing to change these traits in order to become more effective as a leader?" Leadership requires willingness to invest a tremendous amount of personal time to grow and develop the abundance of skills that we currently lack—it's not something that's inborn in anyone.

Leadership When You Don't Know What to Do

The most effective leaders know that the skill that determines success or failure more than any other is the ability to draw on the right inner resources in any given moment. The job of a school leader requires an acute self-awareness in order to decide which trait, characteristic, attribute, or skill is needed to help us navigate a particular situation, problem, or event.

> **The most effective leaders know that the skill that determines success or failure more than any other is the ability to draw on the right inner resources in any given moment.**

Consider this mantra on leadership:

I can be a leader and still ask for help.

I can be confident and still have doubt.

I can expect excellence and still be empathetic.

I can be direct and still be kind.

I can work with urgency and still be patient.

I can be strong and still be vulnerable.

Leadership to me is not only knowing how to use the tools in your toolbox, but knowing how to find the right skill for the job—especially when you don't know exactly what to do.

Your Credibility Is All You Have

I know there were times when I frustrated (and maybe even annoyed) my staff and colleagues, even though I may have had good intentions. But there was always one thing that kept me focused on regrouping quickly every time I took a misstep. I knew that if I were to lose one asset, I would eventually lose my effectiveness as a building leader. That asset? My credibility.

Credibility is what allows us to influence others in a positive way. It instills in others the belief and trust that we are capable of performing at a high level. It opens the door for us to be approachable. Because of credibility, leaders can make change occur more frequently, more effectively, and with less resistance. To lose credibility can spell doomsday for teachers and administrators, especially for those who strive to excel.

There are some things you must do if you want to keep your credibility:

- **Seek solutions.** If you fall short of the outcomes you were hoping for, ask others where they think the plan went sideways, regroup, and then get back to work side by side to achieve your desired result. If you're overwhelmed due to the amount of work coming at you, then ask others for help. Asking for help on the front end is more credible than making excuses on the back end.

- **Share the credit.** Yes, certainly we want to celebrate moments of achievement, but spend more time celebrating the successes of others rather than your own.

- **Admit that you don't know it all.** No one knows everything, and anyone who thinks they do is in for trouble. A colleague and good friend of mine often says that he doesn't have any more answers than the rest of us, but he certainly can share his opinions based on his years of experience. See yourself as a learner, not a knower.

- **Accept feedback.** This is especially true if you ask for feedback or input from others. If you are not prepared to accept the responses that are given to you, then refrain from asking. If you ask for input and the responses are contrary to what you expected, guess what? Good news! Recognize this as a sign that perhaps you asked the right people, because they were willing to tell you what you needed to hear.

- **Always tell the truth.** Enough said.

- **Own the data.** Simply put, fudging numbers in order to shine a brighter light on yourself or your school is just wrong. Be transparent when sharing data. Don't exaggerate the results.

- **Embrace difficult conversations.** When you approach others in challenging moments from a caring place and communicate from the heart, there is a good chance that a burden will be lifted from not only their shoulders but yours as well.

Chapter Sixteen

NAVIGATING DIFFICULT CONVERSATIONS

H ow to respond to people in an organization who are under-performing is one of the biggest challenges facing school leaders. The ability to successfully have a difficult conversation with an underperforming staff member requires a skill set that many new educators lack when they first go into the profession. I was no exception. I hadn't yet developed this critical ability when I completed my degree.

Anyone who has attempted to initiate such conversations can attest to the anxiety and worry that comes from the fear of saying the wrong thing. It feels like with one misstep these conversations can go sideways in a span of seconds. This worry often leads to both teachers and administrators avoiding these necessary conversations all together.

Decisions are being made every day in school districts across America on how to deal with ineffective staff. It takes a tremendous skillset to navigate these types of performance reviews, and it's even more challenging to do so in a way that doesn't risk resulting in a grievance or litigation. Unfortunately, this leads to closed-door meetings, and even then school or district leaders can do more harm than good in the way they manage personnel issues. It's clear this is an issue that's worth examining a bit closer.

Imagine an administrator making the following comment: "That teacher Barb needs to go. She doesn't even like kids. She should have retired five years ago." Frankly, what we're talking about here is not a teacher issue but rather a leadership issue. If Barb has performed her duties at a level most would consider unsatisfactory *for years*, why is she still employed?

The best way—and the only way in my opinion—to move forward is to sit down with Barb and begin discussions regarding her performance. We certainly should not reward Barb by giving her less responsibility, and we should not transfer her to another school so our problems become someone else's problems. Changing classes, teaching schedules, job descriptions, buildings, or even offering early retirement in order to get someone to leave is not only inappropriate but leads to an unhealthy culture. Underperformance by students and staff is going to be an issue, but failing to address underperformance has the potential to become an even bigger one.

One reason why underperformance continues to go unchallenged is because—you guessed it—educators lack the necessary skills for dealing with students and staff who are not performing at the standard expected. How is this possible? Well for one, most educators never received the proper training on addressing poor performance. Think about it. The only in-service training most of us ever received on this topic was from trial and error on the job.

Ask any teacher or principal what challenges they face in their work, and I bet that they would rank their students and staff not performing at the standard they expect somewhere near the top. Other concerns like poor attendance, peers' inability to get along with each other, or dishonesty might rank higher, but I would argue that these are actually much easier to address: they often violate school rules or policies, giving the teacher or supervisor a known path for recourse. But what about the student who you just can't quite figure out because one day they are in class and the next day absent? Or the teacher, administrator, secretary, or school bus driver that simply cannot or will not perform the duties required of them at a high level. Complicating matters is that many times these individuals are "really nice," making it even more difficult for teachers and supervisors to address legitimate concerns regarding underperformance. We cannot continue to run and hide from potential conflict. By doing so, we become passive participants. Our staff deserves better, and we should expect better. We must not allow fear to hold us back.

So what can be done when it comes to dealing with the student or staff member who is underperforming while investing in our culture?

1. **Share your concerns with the individual.** People can't fix what they don't know. Everyone deserves an opportunity to respond to concerns about the quality of their work. Approach the conversation in a genuine, caring, and empathetic manner. People respond best when they believe you truly care about them as people first.

2. **Make feedback more informational than judgmental.** Make your approach more about what you saw from your perspective rather than what the person did wrong. Pay attention to your tone, facial expression, and body language. It all contributes to how feedback is received. Show that you intend to help.

3. **Ask the individual if they agree with your summation.** Don't make assumptions about why you believe they are not meeting expectations. We cannot assume that they are even aware of your or others' concerns. Often people are unaware that their performance has fallen below standard. Other times they are aware, but they cannot even tell you how they ended up there.

4. **Give the individual an opportunity to respond to your concerns.** In some instances, the person may apologize and promise to improve their performance immediately. Others may appear to be caught off guard and respond in a defensive manner. In such cases, be fair by giving them time to process what you have shared and schedule another time to continue the conversation.

5. **Provide specific ways to improve.** This is most helpful to the individual who wants to improve the quality of their work but may be lacking the necessary skills to do so. It's not enough to just tell them they need to get better.

6. **Model the level of performance you expect.** Once you have told the individual what they need to do to raise their level of performance, show them what excellence looks like. Provide a model so they can see it before you expect them to replicate it.

7. **Offer ongoing support.** It is imperative that we invest in our students and employees by providing ongoing coaching in order for them to be inspired to improve their performance. This can be done by you, peers, mentors, colleagues, or even an outside resource.

8. **Provide resources and encouragement.** Don't assume that just because you've followed the above steps that they will be able to maintain their new performance. All of us are prone to falling back to average or below average if we do not have a system in place to monitor and support our continued growth.

9. **Follow up by checking in on a regular basis.** Continue to invest in your students and staff by creating experiences in which your interactions with them go beyond the surface and become more meaningful and personal. Your time together should benefit both of you, and you should

come to understand what they need to thrive in their work. Fostering trusting relationships with your students and staff allows you to set expectations higher.

10. **Be clear in your expectations moving forward.** Every individual must know what is expected of them in order to grow and develop in their role and maximize their potential. It is on us as teachers and leaders to be clear and concise.

11. **Recognize and applaud the efforts of students and staff on a personal and more consistent basis.** After all, we know that people who feel valued and appreciated will always do more than what is expected. But we must also be willing to address our class or team when their efforts slip below the standard we expect. It is our duty and our obligation to do so.

And always have an exit plan. In other words, if you are still concerned that a discussion may be contentious or you are nervous that you may say the wrong thing, be prepared to remove yourself from the conversation in a sincere and apologetic way. Here is an example of what that exit plan may look like:

> I am so sorry if I have upset you. That was not my intention. This is not easy for me either, but I felt it was only fair to bring this matter to your attention. This conversation has not gone the way I hoped it would go, and it is obvious I have not done a very good job of expressing my concerns because I can see that I have upset you, and for that I am truly sorry. I hope you can forgive me. Could we maybe step away from this and start over and have this conversation again?

When it comes to having difficult conversations, don't be afraid to make mistakes. Just own your mistakes, apologize, and ask for forgiveness. Try that the next time you have to have a difficult conversation and it doesn't quite go the way you anticipated. You still may

> # We cannot continue to accept substandard performances by our students, support staff, and teachers, but more importantly, as supervisors and principals we cannot accept substandard performances by ourselves either.

fall short of resolving the issue, but you will be well on your way to developing your skill set for addressing the behaviors that are hurting your culture.

Both students and staff want to know that we care about them. We cannot continue to accept substandard performances from our students, support staff, and teachers, but more importantly, as supervisors and principals we cannot accept substandard performances from ourselves either.

We must always return to the basic premise that it all begins with relationships and the amount of time we are investing in getting to know our students and staff on a more personal level. When we don't have a personal relationship with those who are underperforming in our organizations, we will struggle to manage these conversations effectively. Finally, it is imperative that we live by the mantra that every student and staff member deserves to be treated fairly and to believe that we care about them. We must be hypervigilant not to give harsher penalties to some students and staff because they have a history of poor behavior or performance. So always end with this question to hold yourself to the highest of standards and integrity: would you follow the same steps if you didn't like the person?

What to Do When You Fall Short

I was part of a group discussion where a building principal shared that he had been called to the superintendent's office. He shared that it wasn't the first time he had been called in to have a talk, but this time just the tone of the superintendent's voice made him a bit nervous about why the meeting was being called. That got me to thinking how we behave as building and district leaders when it comes to managing conversations.

As a building or district leader, here are a few things you might want to consider stopping today:

- **Calling staff to your office without offering an explanation of what the meeting will entail.** This causes a person's anxiety level to increase. From the moment they receive notice, their mind will begin to swirl with possibilities of what the meeting is about. And in most cases, people will think the worst.
- **Giving excuses when you fail to follow up.** Understand that when you don't get back to people in a timely fashion it gives others the impression that you are not organized or, in some instances, that their needs are not important to you.

- **Talking negatively about your staff to other staff.** Speaking negatively about others actually says more about you than it does about the people you are singling out. This also leads to mistrust among staff, as it will inevitably get back to others that you are talking about them in a negative light.
- **Allowing people in your school to bully other staff.** We cannot cultivate a high-performing learning environment in our schools if staff is intimidating their own colleagues through their words or actions.
- **Using the word "they" when referring to other members of your school community**, especially when things are not going well or we are not happy about an outcome. Focus more on "we" when celebrating something positive or trying to work through any significant challenge.
- **Making assumptions.** It is never a good idea to go into a conversation or a situation believing you know more than you actually do. This has the potential to create trust issues, so avoid doing so at all costs.
- **Getting frustrated when you think people are not following your directions.** Begin by asking yourself if you have provided enough clarity. Were your directions as clear as they could have been?
- **Expecting everything to go as planned.** Working in schools can sometimes be unpredictable because the variables (students and teachers) are always changing. How you conduct yourself in these moments will either inspire or deflate your team.

- **Responding to harsh and not-so-complimentary emails with your own.** Recognize that others' moments of frustration, blame, or accusatory language are often more about other external factors and can have nothing to do with you. Pick up the phone and call the person and ask, "What can I do to ease your frustration or disappointment?"
- **Asking your staff for feedback and then not doing anything with it.** If your staff gets frustrated because they don't think you did anything with the feedback and you think you did, reflect on how you could have communicated more effectively so they would know the progress you're making with the information they provided you.
- **Addressing matters of concern to an entire faculty when only a few are not meeting the expectations you've set forth.** Often everyone else knows who the violators are, but the violators themselves don't realize you are referring to them. Your best staff members will resent you for wasting their time. Always address violators individually.
- **Being a critic.** Challenging the status quo is one thing, but to change it requires us to commit on a different level. It is easy to be a critic and a talker, but it's another thing to be a doer. Believe that a group of talented people can come together and find a way to make it happen.

Thinking Differently about Parents

I've always believed that education is an obligation that should be shared between the school, a child's guardians, students, and the community. My experience working with parents over the years was overwhelmingly positive. The majority of parents that I worked with were kind, generous, and committed to supporting the school in their quest to provide the best learning experiences for all students. Without the support of parents, we would be extremely hard pressed to meet all of the expectations required of us as educators. More often than not, parents want to be part of the solution. They give freely of their time, energy, expertise, and resources when needed. However, sometimes the same passion that fuels a fire to provide the best experiences for their own child fuels a different kind of fire, the kind that burns hottest when they feel their student has been wronged in some way.

Over the years, I've encountered my share of upset parents. At times some of them were livid and some were so upset they seemed to be on the brink of losing their minds. Stay in this profession long enough and you will eventually share a similar experience—I assure you. We can argue whether or not we should have to tolerate such aggressive and inappropriate behavior, but we can be sure of two things: parents have a right to show up for their children, and we should expect them to advocate for them.

I have spent a lot of time reflecting on this topic as I work with educators who continue to struggle with how to deal with parents who are upset with a staff member, the school, or the system in general. Threats of bodily harm, lawsuits, and social media posts asking for the removal of a teacher or principal are not uncommon responses these days from parents who wish to voice their displeasure with school personnel. We are expected to be prepared to manage such volatile situations in an era when threats to staff are real and sometimes carried out. Yet, we forge ahead trying to navigate these situations because we believe it is our professional duty. This has all led me to a new line of thinking on the matter.

Parents don't get upset at us because they don't like us or they hate us, they get upset at us because they care about us and they like us. Huh? Parents scream and curse at us because they like us? Maybe.

Imagine sitting on the couch watching your favorite athlete or sports team play poorly. You are not only upset because your team is losing, you're angry at the way they are playing. But you still love your team and your favorite athlete. That's kind of a like an upset parent who is disappointed at the way they perceive their child's school performing. You see, we root for those we love, and at times we talk negatively about them when they don't meet our expectations or disappoint us. On occasion, parents will behave in the same manner toward us. When the next week rolls around, we show up for our team, ready to cheer for them again. Our team forgives us for the way we behaved previously, and we believe that they'll do better this time around. Parents are upset because they care and because they feel connected. That's a good thing, right? They are passionate about their children and their schools, and this influences their behavior.

So when should we worry? When they just accept poor results without incident. Because in that moment they either think it is not worth it, they no longer care, or they've realized that nothing is ever going to change and they've decided to move on to a new team (or in our case a new school). Either way, we lose. We lose due to apathy— the enemy of hope.

And hope is all we got when it comes to connecting with angry parents. Maybe it's time to think about parents' behavior differently. If all we can say is "that parent is crazy" or "they aren't ever going to change so why bother," then perhaps we are the ones talking crazy and the ones who are reluctant to change.

Don't Apologize for Caring

A principal in Wisconsin had just gotten word from the central office that a great counselor at his school was going to be transferred to another school. He was disappointed.

Regrettably, scenarios like this play out far too often. Staff members are told late in the school year that their contracts are not being renewed for the following year. RIF (reduction in force), that acronym that no one wants to hear, is bandied about at school districts throughout the country each year. If you have ever been on the receiving end of news like this, you know the consternation this three-letter word can cause.

To make thing worse, he did not agree with the way the situation was being handled by the district. He was told that he had to keep the information private until the district sent out an email notifying all staff of the upcoming changes for the following year. He couldn't even tell the news to the counselor. She'd have to be kept in the dark about a major change to her job.

The principal was upset. "How can we treat an individual who has given so much to the students, staff, and families in such a disrespectful way?" he thought to himself. "Wouldn't it be better to communicate this decision ASAP rather than wait? And shouldn't this news come in the form of a one-on-one conversation rather than an email?" What was most disturbing was that the principal, who had built an important professional relationship with the counselor, was not allowed to give her the news himself. He couldn't understand treating a staff member—a colleague, friend, wife, mother, and daughter—with such coldness.

Two weeks later the news came out, and as you can imagine, it hit the school counselor like a ton of bricks. The principal went directly to her office to apologize. He felt terrible, and he shared with the counselor how he deeply regretted not only that she was being transferred but how it had been handled. He felt awful and told the counselor that she deserved to be treated better and he wished that he could reverse the decision. She knew his message was heartfelt because it was delivered with tears in his eyes.

You might be thinking that it seems odd that the principal would share all of these intimate details with me. The answer is he didn't have to. That principal was me.

The way we manage (or in some cases mismanage) personnel issues can exasperate feelings of negativity among staff who are both directly and indirectly impacted by our decisions. It is during these times more than ever when we need to give grace and make sure we conduct ourselves in a manner that shows others a model of excellence.

That incident taught me many valuable lessons about the simple truths of leadership. The most important one came from the counselor, whose name was Erin. She had been given every reason to be upset and resentful of everyone who had been involved in the RIF decision and to be hurt about the way the situation had been handled. Instead, her response taught me the most valuable lesson of all. As I sat there nervously waiting for her reaction (I was sure it would be loaded with bitterness), Erin looked at me and said, "Don't ever apologize for caring."

And with these five words, she reminded me that when people feel valued and cared for, their personal excellence will rise above their moments of disappointment.

Invest in Excellence for Everyone

Many of our teachers and principals entering our schools today believe they are prepared for the demands the job will entail. The problem is that in today's workplace it doesn't take long for people to wonder about our skills and competence. Before you even realize it, the whispers become apparent and people begin to question our effectiveness and our ability to do our jobs. Some schools have frameworks and support systems in place to better equip their staff with the right tools and skill sets to help them experience more success as they begin their tenure, but what about those that don't? It's great when schools and districts perform well and see their staff and students benefit from such support systems. Unless you are one of those schools or educators not receiving the same level of support. Ultimately this is an equity issue, which is why I feel so strongly that we must carry the banner not only for our students, teachers, and schools but for our profession as a whole. We need to advocate for putting support systems into place that will benefit all kids as well as every adult and volunteer who works in our schools.

When I set out to write this book, I wanted to share some of the truths that I have learned in my twenty-six-year career in education. I also aimed to challenge you to see yourself from a different perspective regardless of your role in school to show you how you, as one individual, can influence the thinking and behavior of another individual.

My hope was for you to aspire to invest in students, colleagues, and most of all yourself in order to elevate your own actions, responses, and behaviors to a higher level. I also wanted my words to give every educator working in schools today some insight into how to carefully navigate the pitfalls of compliance.

I felt compelled to share with you where I fell short in my efforts and to allow you to see my deficiencies and failures in order to hopefully inspire you to do the same with others. We cannot and should not allow our shortcomings to define our work, our impact, or our success.

The work of an educator is extremely challenging, which is why I think we need to continue to put support systems into place that focus on coaching educators so they can identify and anticipate where a compliance mindset will emerge. Ms. Silver didn't see it, but Antwan did eventually. It fooled him initially when Ms. Silver offered him a reward, but he saw it for what it was—disingenuous—and it backfired on her. I sat on the edge of the couch in tears twelve years into my career as a principal wanting to quit because I couldn't see the culture of compliance that I had created.

When I look back on my career I now understand that I was not prepared for the all of the situations I would encounter both as a teacher and as a principal. I have forgiven myself for my past mistakes, and today I am committed to simply trying to better myself in every aspect of my life, including trying to help others navigate the same treacherous undercurrents of compliance I was once responsible for. I strongly encourage you to reflect on your past and do the same, but don't be too hard on yourself. Accept that there will be days when you are left to discern what is true and what is fake. No degree can ever prepare you for the challenges that will come your way, but you can shift your mindset and begin to believe that you can inspire others to new heights.

When you decide that you are ready, embrace your vulnerability and strive to live your excellence in both your professional and personal life.

Reflecting on Excellence

- What processes does your organization currently have in place to collect feedback from all stakeholders? How are results communicated to everyone? How is progress monitored and communicated and how often does this happen?

- Reflect on the following claim: "Leadership is not about having positional power over someone but having relational influence on them."

- What are three ways a culture of investment makes difficult conversations easier than a culture of compliance?

- What processes could we put in place to make sure that when we are faced with unique or difficult situations with students, colleagues, or parents our response is seen as fair and equitable?

CONCLUSION

AT THE END OF THIS TEACHING LIFE ALL I WILL
HAVE IS WHAT I'VE LEFT BEHIND ME.
–PAUL STEFFAN

In the early nineties my family lived on the south side of Milwaukee in a small two-bedroom apartment. We had recently moved away from a nicer part of town in order to try and make ends meet. As many educators can attest to, the first few years on the job can be stressful for any young family trying to make ends meet, so even the $125 monthly rental savings brought some relief to our financial burdens. We were young, blessed, and full of (some would say) "idealistic" dreams and hopes for the future. My wife stayed home with our toddler, Aj, and volunteered at the Exchange Center, mentoring a teen mom with two kids. I was working at an inner-city middle school.

It was not the type of school where all of the parents packed their kids' lunches, dropped them off at the door, and waited eagerly that evening to hear about their day. Most of these preteens got themselves out of bed and boarded a city bus at the crack of dawn. The administration would raffle off television sets just to improve attendance at parent-teacher conference nights.

One night our apartment became more full when three young children took up residence in our living room. Justin was an eleven-year-old student of mine. Sitting next to Justin were his two siblings, Chimera and Chelsea, ages twelve and seven. Over the course of the school year, I had become personally invested in Justin. As his teacher, I was drawn to his story based on what he, the social worker, and the school administration had shared with me. I knew his dad was not in the picture and his mom had her own significant challenges she was trying to deal with at the time. My wife and I had convinced ourselves that it was our calling to save these kids from their environment. We were determined to make a difference, and we truly believed that we could. Suffice it to say that it was a different time: our actions, although well intentioned, would certainly not be encouraged today. Justin regularly ate dinner in our home, spent holidays with our family, and even joined us for camping trips back to Iowa.

Earlier one evening we traveled to the north side of Milwaukee to pick Justin up, as we had many times before, and found him home alone with his two sisters. The kids shared some information with us that made us concerned for their safety, so we loaded them all up and took them home. In the span of a few hours, our worries about Justin shifted to a much greater concern—the safety and well-being of all three kids not just for this one night but for each night moving forward.

The kids spent the evening on our living room floor as we called the Department of Human Services. We even discussed fostering these precious children because we couldn't think of anyone better than ourselves to raise three kids—in addition to our own. In that moment we disregarded the big picture. We couldn't comprehend why we wouldn't be the better choice to raise these kids over their own mother. We couldn't understand why Justin was so angry at us for calling DHS. And we certainly could not accept the fact that we could not "save" these kids.

As you might imagine, we did not end up fostering three kids, and Justin did not make a high school commencement speech thanking me for all of my valiant efforts. In fact, Justin did not even graduate. He went to prison.

Over the years I observed and tried to counsel other teachers and administrators on the perils of trying to go down the dangerous road of trying to save kids. I understood their reasons for wanting to do it and empathized with them. For many educators, this is our core, it's who we are, and often it defines our entire purpose for becoming an educator. It is how we define our success. Those of you who have a similar motivation may understand why I tried to define my success by how many kids I was impacting in any given year.

The problem is, I wasn't sure what success really looked like. Impact? How do I measure that? If you would have asked me back in the early nineties, I would have told you I lost one. Lost him to the streets. To drugs. To the gangs. To the system and eventually prison.

I reconnected with Justin in high school. I was now a building administrator, and he had reached out to me hoping to get another chance at school. In many ways, he was still that cocky little eleven-year-old with a million-dollar smile that warmed my heart whenever I looked at him. He reminded me so much of myself at that age I couldn't help but be drawn to him. Yes, he still had a lot of kid in him, but he was now a young man of sixteen years of age. He was more guarded now, hardened by the broken promises from the adults in his life. His second tenure in school was short lived. He couldn't assimilate back into the life of a full-time student and eventually gave up and quit. I remember feeling like I had let him down, wondering how his life would have been different had we just committed to taking him in back when he was eleven. In my heart, I felt like I had failed him.

Over the years, although our lives would take us in different directions causing us to lose touch with one another, I never stopped thinking about him. How could I? He impacted my life and gave me the tools through our interactions, our talks, our challenges, to help me become a better teacher, a better principal. Yet, that sinking feeling that I had failed him never left me.

About ten years ago, I received a letter in the mail from Justin. He was in prison. His wife had contacted me and gave me a phone number with visiting hours where I could call him. I was nervous and excited at the same time. When I heard his voice for the first time, all I could see was that face from sixth grade looking at me in class. After twenty minutes, my spirits had been lifted, a void in my heart filled. He said some things to me that day that made be believe that maybe, just maybe, I had made a small impact. That I wasn't fake.

I wish I could tell you that we reconnected that day in a way that brought us back together, teacher and student. Fairytale ending. But it didn't happen. I don't even know why. Maybe we just needed that one final conversation to move on with our lives. After all, both of us were dealing with our own issues. Regardless, the timing just didn't work.

The old version of me would have beat myself up over it. No more. I know this one thing: During the time I had Justin as a student, I gave him all I had. There were times I recall being questioned by other teachers and administrators about what I was getting for my return on investment with this kid. Honestly, I wasn't really sure how to answer that question, other than to say that I knew in my heart that someday my efforts would make a difference. I didn't know how, but I believed it.

If you have had a similar experience with a student, you get what I am saying here. A relationship with a kid can grab you by the heart, and you find yourself not able to let go. Not if you want to leave your mark. Sometimes, for teachers the dividends don't come until much later. When we focus on the now, we often feel like we've been short-changed. Like we didn't make a difference. Like we weren't successful.

I often think of counselors who work in treatment facilities. When a patient relapses has the counselor failed? I don't think so. As they invest in that relationship they are making a difference. Their words make a difference. The coping skills they teach their patients make a difference. The hope that things can be better makes a difference. Counselors, just like educators, must recognize that what they are doing is making a difference in some small way and that investments in others might not yield a return in some cases until years later.

You've experienced it. One day when you least expect it you get a surprise email from a former student, and it warms your heart. Or you run into a family in the grocery store and recognize one of the parents as a former student and they share a story with you or give you a sincere thank you for everything you did for them. You probably don't remember most of what they remember. But they remember.

And sometimes that long-lost student never gives up on you and reaches out in his moment of need and says, "I told the pastor there was one person who has always been there for me when I needed him and that is you." This young man, this survivor, after all of his ordeals, at the age of thirty-nine is asked by his pastor if there is anyone in his life that made an impact on him that could serve as a mentor and be there for him in his darkest moments. Anyone that he would feel comfortable reaching out to. And who does he think of? His teacher from sixth grade. That could be any one of us. It could be you!

Justin and I reconnected via Facebook this past year. This time I have vowed things will be different. I will not allow myself to lose touch with him again as long as he wants to have a relationship with his former teacher and principal. He sounds good, healthy, and ready to make the necessary changes in order to avoid any more incarceration. He knows there will be challenges. He admitted to me that he at times is drawn to revert back to the "old" Justin because with the old Justin comes a reputation that can benefit him, but he also understands that it can hurt him. He has told me that he will not let his past failures define his future success.

I don't plan to allow Justin's time in prison to define my impact or my success and I hope you won't allow the past failures of some of your students to define yours either. I know there are days when you question whether it's all worth it or you allow other people's words to influence your thinking on whether or not you can save them all. In those moments when doubt begins to creep in remember, there is a Justin out there who just might remind you that on any given day you can change the course of a student's life through your belief in them and redefine success for both of you.

Reflecting on Excellence

- Let go of those who have wronged you in some way, and forgive those who have hurt you with their words or actions. Don't spend your energy scanning the world for the negatives, and don't let the anyone hijack your positivity.

- Develop an attitude of gratitude to remind you of the abundance of blessings that surround you. Always believe that something wonderful is about to happen.

- Rather than see things happening *to* you, begin to see things happening *for* you. Every interaction, experience, and moment in your day is progress toward a life lived without regret and a life fulfilled.

ACKNOWLEDGMENTS

I would like to thank Dave and Shelley Burgess for their continued friendship, unconditional support, and persistent encouragement to share my story and life's work. It has been an honor and a blessing to work with the entire DBC team. Thanks to Sal for your never-ending patience, positivity, and insight in supporting me to bring this book to print. To George, Jeff, Joe, and Tom, thank you for your unwavering friendship. You four make me a better educator, speaker, and writer and a better friend. Finally, thank you Justin for showing me and all educators that on any given day one student can reignite the passion for teaching and give us hope by reminding us to be grateful for the abundance of blessings that we have been given.

MORE FROM

Dave Burgess Consulting, inc.

Since 2012, DBCI has been publishing books that inspire and equip educators to be their best. For more information on our DBCI titles or to purchase bulk orders for your school, district, or book study, visit **DaveBurgessConsulting.com/DBCIbooks**.

More Leadership & School Culture

Culturize by Jimmy Casas

Escaping the School Leader's Dunk Tank by Rebecca Coda and Rick Jetter

From Teacher to Leader by Starr Sackstein

The Innovator's Mindset by George Couros

It's OK to Say "They" by Christy Whittlesey

Kids Deserve It! by Todd Nesloney and Adam Welcome

Let Them Speak by Rebecca Coda and Rick Jetter

The Limitless School by Abe Hege and Adam Dovico

The Pepper Effect by Sean Gaillard

The Principled Principal by Jeffrey Zoul and Anthony McConnell

Relentless by Hamish Brewer

The Secret Solution by Todd Whitaker, Sam Miller, and Ryan Donlan

Start. Right. Now. by Todd Whitaker, Jeffrey Zoul, and Jimmy Casas

Stop. Right. Now. by Jimmy Casas and Jeffrey Zoul

They Call Me "Mr. De" by Frank DeAngelis

Unmapped Potential by Julie Hasson and Missy Lennard

Word Shift by Joy Kirr

Your School Rocks by Ryan McLane and Eric Lowe

Lead Like a PIRATE™ Series

Lead Like a PIRATE by Shelley Burgess and Beth Houf

Balance Like a Pirate by Jessica Cabeen, Jessica Johnson, and Sarah Johnson

Lead beyond Your Title by Nili Bartley

Lead with Appreciation by Amber Teamann and Melinda Miller

Lead with Culture by Jay Billy

Lead with Literacy by Mandy Ellis

Like a PIRATE™ Series

Teach Like a PIRATE by Dave Burgess

eXPlore Like a Pirate by Michael Matera

Learn Like a Pirate by Paul Solarz

Play Like a Pirate by Quinn Rollins

Run Like a Pirate by Adam Welcome

Technology & Tools

50 Things You Can Do with Google Classroom by Alice Keeler and Libbi Miller

50 Things to Go Further with Google Classroom by Alice Keeler and Libbi Miller

140 Twitter Tips for Educators by Brad Currie, Billy Krakower, and Scott Rocco

Block Breaker by Brian Aspinall

Code Breaker by Brian Aspinall

Google Apps for Littles by Christine Pinto and Alice Keeler

Master the Media by Julie Smith

Reality Bytes by Christine Lion-Bailey, Jesse Lubinsky, and Micah Shippee, PhD

Shake Up Learning by Kasey Bell

Social LEADia by Jennifer Casa-Todd

Teaching Math with Google Apps by Alice Keeler and Diana Herrington

Teachingland by Amanda Fox and Mary Ellen Weeks

Teaching Methods & Materials

All 4s and 5s by Andrew Sharos

Boredom Busters by Katie Powell

The Classroom Chef by John Stevens and Matt Vaudrey

The Collaborative Classroom by Trevor Muir

Copyrighteous by Diana Gill

Ditch That Homework by Matt Miller and Alice Keeler

Ditch That Textbook by Matt Miller

Don't Ditch That Tech by Matt Miller, Nate Ridgway, and Angelia Ridgway

EDrenaline Rush by John Meehan

Educated by Design by Michael Cohen, The Tech Rabbi

The EduProtocol Field Guide by Marlena Hebern and Jon Corippo

The EduProtocol Field Guide: Book 2 by Marlena Hebern and Jon Corippo

Instant Relevance by Denis Sheeran

LAUNCH by John Spencer and A. J. Juliani

Make Learning MAGICAL by Tisha Richmond

Pure Genius by Don Wettrick

The Revolution by Darren Ellwein and Derek McCoy

Shift This! by Joy Kirr

Spark Learning by Ramsey Musallam

Sparks in the Dark by Travis Crowder and Todd Nesloney

Table Talk Math by John Stevens

The Wild Card by Hope and Wade King

The Writing on the Classroom Wall by Steve Wyborney

Inspiration, Professional Growth & Personal Development

Be REAL by Tara Martin

Be the One for Kids by Ryan Sheehy

The Coach ADVenture by Amy Illingworth

Creatively Productive by Lisa Johnson

Educational Eye Exam by Alicia Ray

The EduNinja Mindset by Jennifer Burdis

Empower Our Girls by Lynmara Colón and Adam Welcome

Finding Lifelines by Andrew Grieve and Andrew Sharos

The Four O'Clock Faculty by Rich Czyz

How Much Water Do We Have? by Pete and Kris Nunweiler

P Is for Pirate by Dave and Shelley Burgess

A Passion for Kindness by Tamara Letter

The Path to Serendipity by Allyson Apsey

Sanctuaries by Dan Tricarico

The SECRET SAUCE by Rich Czyz

Shattering the Perfect Teacher Myth by Aaron Hogan

Stories from Webb by Todd Nesloney

Talk to Me by Kim Bearden

Teach Better by Chad Ostrowski, Tiffany Ott, Rae Hughart, and Jeff Gargas

Teach Me, Teacher by Jacob Chastain

TeamMakers by Laura Robb and Evan Robb

Through the Lens of Serendipity by Allyson Apsey

The Zen Teacher by Dan Tricarico

Children's Books

Beyond Us by Aaron Polansky

Cannonball In by Tara Martin

Dolphins in Trees by Aaron Polansky

I Want to Be a Lot by Ashley Savage

The Princes of Serendip by Allyson Apsey

The Wild Card Kids by Hope and Wade King

Zom-Be a Design Thinker by Amanda Fox

ABOUT THE AUTHOR

Jimmy Casas served twenty-two years as a school leader, including fourteen years as principal at Bettendorf High School. Under his leadership, Bettendorf was named one of the best high schools in the country three times by *Newsweek* and *U.S. News & World Report.*

Jimmy was named the 2012 Iowa Secondary Principal of the Year and was selected as one of three finalists for NASSP 2013 National Secondary Principal of the Year. In 2014, Jimmy was invited to the White House to speak on the Future Ready Schools pledge. Jimmy is also the author of four previous books, *What Connected Educators Do Differently*, *Start. Right. Now.: Teach and Lead for Excellence*, the best-selling book *Culturize: Every Student. Every Day. Whatever It Takes*, and *Stop. Right. Now.: The 39 Stops to Making Schools Better.*

Jimmy currently serves as an adjunct professor for Drake University, teaching courses in educational leadership. Finally, he is the owner and CEO of J Casas & Associates, an educational leadership company aimed at organizing and providing world-class professional learning services for educators across the country.

CPSIA information can be obtained
at www.ICGtesting.com
Printed in the USA
JSHW041542220522
26069JS00004B/20